Be Authentic

Be Authentic

THREE KEYS TO UNLOCKING YOUR TRUE POTENTIAL

ELAINE K. HARDING, PhD

BALBOA
PRESS
A DIVISION OF HAY HOUSE

Balboa Press books may be ordered through booksellers or by contacting:

Balboa Press
A Division of Hay House
1663 Liberty Drive
Bloomington, IN 47403
www.balboapress.com.au
1-(877) 407-4847

ISBN: 978-1-4525-1109-2 (sc)
ISBN: 978-1-4525-1110-8 (e)

Printed in the United States of America

Balboa Press rev. date: 09/09/2013

This book is dedicated to my dear sister Rachele, whose life and death inspired me to recognise that the authentic source of abundance is within and ever present.

Standing naked
atop a glacier,
Sun soft on my face
Fear below, sky unblue
Freedom

—Elaine K. Harding

It takes
courage
to grow up
and become
who you really are.

—*e.e. cummings*

Contents

Acknowledgements..xi

Introduction   **The Flow of Being Authentic** xiii

Chapter 1   **The Judgemental K(not)s that Limit the Flow**... 1

Chapter 2   **Key 1 – Reset: Move from Rejection to Acceptance of Your Emotions and Experiences**.................... 11
You Have to Feel to Heal....................... 15
An Empathic Welcome Mat 20
Call Off the Search Party...................... 23
Accender 28
Practices for Chapter 2 34

Chapter 3   **Key 2 – Reconnect: Claim Your Authentic Being**................................... 37
Embrace Dignity..................................... 43
Value Yourself, Value Others.................. 49
Strategies Are K(not) Needs................... 54
Be Real, Act with Zeal........................... 57

Carry Tissues and a Wrench 62

Practices for Chapter 3 68

Chapter 4   **Key 3 – Release: Let Go to Let
Your Authentic Life Flow** 71

Trust.. 74

Life Is But a Dream! 78

Be Naked, Be Forgiving............................ 81

Life Is a Flow, Let It All Go 86

Practices for Chapter 4 90

Chapter 5   **Living an Authentic Life** 93

About the Author...................................... 97

Bibliography... 99

Acknowledgements

The beginnings of this book arrived in my heart early in 2009, like seeds being planted in my subconscious. As the year progressed, the person I had imagined myself to be dissolved into an unrecognizable heap of ashes. And within that fertile ground, the seeds remained unharmed. As my mind and body healed, these seeds took root and grew quietly and strongly until I was ready to allow their wisdom to pour forth into this book. For this experience, for my constantly unfolding and amazing life, and for the guidance and ever-present love from the Divine Source—for all these I am deeply grateful.

My journey back to my authentic self was accelerated by my interactions with, and learning from, Marshall B. Rosenberg, Chöygal Namkhai Norbu, and all of my dharma friends. To my dear friends Kelly Barry, Mary Wagner, Ruth Zee, Dammika Pereira, Rod Marland, Rosemary Hill, Jacqui Balston, and Nerissa Brandenberger, I am forever thankful for all of your encouragement, strength, and immense kindness over the years.

My partner Harry inspires me with his laughter and enduring love, and I am deeply grateful to him for his support in allowing me to live my dreams. And my sincere appreciation also goes to my brother, Greg Harding, who maintained a belief in me even when I temporarily could not.

I am thankful to the following people who generously gave of their time in reading the early drafts of this book: Ruth Zee, Jill Knell, and Kelli Harris. And thanks to the editor at Balboa Press and to my editor, Glyn Davies, who was able to discipline and bring to life any badly behaved words that I had written.

I also appreciate the support and advice given by the staff at Balboa Press and to Christine Kloser, the inspirational host of the Transformational Author series whose enthusiasm ignited in me a desire to publish this book so that others may find their way home again.

INTRODUCTION

The Flow of Being Authentic

I sense that you and I both yearn for the same ultimate experience: for our lives to be a constant flow of love, trust, and joy. However, our daily realities don't always seem to meet this higher expectation, and you, like me, have probably felt a strong urge to work out why. Then you picked up this book, wondering if it might just give you a few clues.

My wish for you in reading this book is that you will begin to fully experience an authentic life—a life filled with an uninterrupted flow of love, trust, and joy. As children, we experienced this flow as naturally as the sun shines down on the earth. A feeling of love and acceptance moved naturally through our hearts and minds, and if anything interrupted it, we would cry, shout, and let our feelings out and then be back to being in the flow again.

Throughout this book, I use the terms "being authentic" and "the flow of an authentic life" to express the deeper energetic connection that comes from surrendering to and enjoying what is present in this moment of now. Of course, what is present may feel pleasurable, but other times it may not. Authenticity does not equal pleasure; rather, it points towards a more profound acceptance of the movement of life and its continual state of change as applied to our mental, physical, and emotional worlds. It's about a sense of strong alignment with the truth of the moment.

The strongest influence on our current sense of well-being and acceptance is our past and, in particular, how we learned to conceptualise our experiences when we were children. When we were very young, we experienced the delightful present moment as a never-ending flow of positive energy; therefore, any events that appeared to stop this flow had a strong impact on us. Around these events we began to create stories that reflected what each of us believed could be the cause of the bad feeling, or what I call the k(not) in our flow—the story that says this should not be happening. Our minds always attempt to make sense of life and, if we are troubled, our minds try to soothe us with stories. For example, in childhood, we'd say things like "Johnny is being selfish," or "Kim is bad-tempered," or even "I must be bad because I talk too much in class." The story or label helped us justify what was happening, and then we could get back to life again.

Those simple stories that we began telling ourselves, and the ones that others in our immediate families told us, reinforced the view that objects external to us and our own behaviours, were the cause of the flow stopping. Our minds filed away these stories, especially those with a strong emotional content. Now, in the present, their essential features are remembered even more than the incident that provoked them in the past. For example, when I was nine years old, I saw a brown bear for the first time while camping with my best friend's family. The feeling associated with it was "excitement and awe," and I can still feel those emotions when I think about the incident today, although I can't recall much about the event's details. My story about that incident is this: "Seeing bears is an exciting and awe-inspiring experience."

Although my story about this particular bear may have been true, does that mean that every future experience with a bear would be the same for me? For about ten years after that initial encounter, I had several more exciting experiences when seeing bears, so my mind continued to reinforce my story. Then my experiences began to change. When I took up backpacking around the age of twenty, I became annoyed by the theft of my precious food by the mongrel bears! The story had changed. It now became: "Bears are menaces, and I would rather not have them nearby."

So, stories can reinforce a certain feeling in us even before we experience a future event. This occurs because of the link between our stories' content and particular emotions, especially the stronger and more negatively charged emotions, such as anger, fear, and depression. These create very deep connections to our stories.

The flow of being authentic is stopped or slowed down when we totally believe our stories, repress our emotions, and stop accepting and trusting life. The flow returns when we go back to the origins of our stories and release the blocked emotions that we didn't originally express. When we feel the emotions fully from those original events, rather than reacting in our habitual way, the flow starts moving through us again. Yet, we don't often allow this natural release to occur. The fact is that whenever we re-experience the original emotions, we often choose to push them down and continue to believe in our stories instead of letting the full range of our feelings emerge to be dealt with once and for all.

Why push down original emotions when, if we simply released them, the flow would start again? The answer is both simple and complex. Simple, in that if we did allow them to be fully released, there would be no block to the flow. Complexity comes into the scene, however, because we begin to use our brains to *analyse* the situation, to *explain* what has happened. Our *thoughts* then become the explanation for what has happened, and these *replace and block the emotion*. Our authentic feelings are a natural release of energy, yet as we grow up, we are told not to cry, not to shout, not to let our feelings out! In short, we are told to repress our feelings.

Instead of releasing our feelings safely—which means without judgement—we enter into judgement with our feelings. Everyone can remember a scene where their parents or another significant adult first told them that it was inappropriate to show an emotion, saying things like, "Boys don't cry," or "Stop being such a baby." Well, there it is! We've been taught to repress our natural emotions, because as children we were instructed that they were not appropriate for when we grew up.

One of the most fascinating aspects of emotional repression is how deeply it has become embedded into our society. I was trained as a scientist, and the behavioural norm that was modelled—in the background, quite indirectly—was that being a good scientist meant being objective and not emotional. Objectivity implied that we would be removed from our emotional core, and, so went the concept, we would become more rational and able to function from an unbiased perspective. That world view was so ingrained in me during my studies that I didn't question it until just a few days before I completed my PhD.

At that time, I was walking on the campus of the university, and I noticed that my head felt enormous while the remainder of my body was like a stick—or worse, almost non-existent. It was a strange sensation, and it made me acutely aware of how I had almost completely lost contact with my bodily senses. The intellect had virtually taken over my identity.

Many years later, after embarking on a path to rediscover my whole being, I read a book titled *Descartes' Error: Emotion, Reason and the Human Brain* by Antonio R. Damasio (1994). Damasio is a neuroscientist whose studies into brain function led him to discover that without emotion, reasoning cannot operate. Let me say this again. He concluded that if a person lost his capacity to feel emotions, then he also lost his ability to make rational decisions. This concept seemed revolutionary, yet it didn't get much press either in the media or in scientific circles at the time. However, science is one of those disciplines in which paradigms change very slowly, and any change is dependent upon both a strong weight of evidence and a will to shift the consensus position. Not surprisingly, the proposed positive link between emotion and reason has yet to permeate the cracks of the scientific paradigm, which, instead, continues to posit an opposite relationship.

The purpose of this diversion about science and reason is to emphasise that our current Western view of reality is largely derived from the laws of science, and that means that repressing emotion is an expected and frequently reinforced behaviour. Even in the softer scientific fields, such as psychology, it could be thought of as a weakness if psychologists were to show their emotions while with clients. It's as though emotions are so terrifying that they must be kept under constant surveillance, and if there is an attempted breakout, they are quickly escorted back to the cell block!

If emotional release is generally deemed to be unacceptable in adults (with a few noted exceptions, such as crying at funerals and aggression at sporting events), then are there consequent detriments to our well-being from this repression? Western science is now beginning to address this new area of research by asking: 1) how does our thinking impact our emotions, and 2) how does emotional repression influence the health of the physical body? Importantly, different forms of Eastern medicine, as far as I can ascertain, are more advanced in their understanding. Indian, Chinese, and Tibetan medical models all point to important relationships between our emotional, mental, and physical components, although their models are still being integrated into the current Western scientific view of human health.

An example of an alternative perspective is that our human body is also an energy field, and this corresponds to an Eastern medical view indicating the existence of chakras (energy centres) that permeate the body. As natural therapies become more integrated into mainstream society, these models of the human energy system are also gaining wider acceptance. Well-regarded healer and best-selling author Barbara Ann Brennan, who also trained in the Western sciences, provides some relevant insights into the role of thought, emotions, and the flow of energy in the body in relation to our overall well-being.

In her book, *Light Emerging* (1993), Brennan helps us answer these questions regarding emotions and our well-being. The relevant sections of her book are quoted below (with the interesting points that she makes in reference to the consequences of maintaining blocked emotions indicated in italics, and my comments following):

The second level is associated with your feelings or emotions about yourself . . . . *If you allow the feelings about yourself to flow, whether they are negative or positive, the aura keeps itself balanced.* And the negative feelings and the negative energies associated with your feelings are released and transformed. If you stop yourself from having emotions about yourself, you stop the flow of energy in the second level that corresponds to those emotions . . . .

Most of us do not allow all our feelings about ourselves to flow. As a result, most of us have stagnated energy in our second levels and have interfered with our health to varying degrees. (Brennan 1993)

The point that Brennan is making here is that unexpressed emotions get caught in our energy systems, which then create dysfunction in our well-being, as further described in the next section.

The third level is associated with our mental or rational world . . . .

When our thoughts are negative, the pulsations in the field are slower, the lines become dark and distorted. These "negative thought forms" are the form that corresponds to our habitual negative thought processes. They are difficult to change, because they appear to be logical to the person experiencing them. (Brennan 1993)

This is a very important point about "negative thought forms." A thought or a feeling is simply an energy form, and if negative feelings and thoughts are generally unexpressed—even if just to ourselves—they block the flow of energy in our mind and in our body.

> *Another way to understand this is to remember that the natural state of energy is constant movement.* When the movement of energy is stopped in the second and fourth levels in order to stop negative emotions, some of that momentum is transferred into the third level. The momentum that moves into the third level causes mental activity.
> (Brennan 1993)

To understand this point, we need to remember that the second-level aura is feelings about ourselves, and the fourth is our feelings about other people. If we have repressed emotions on both levels, this creates a squeeze effect on level three, our mental activities, meaning we continue to put excessive energy into rational problem solving for issues that actually require a different solution. The solution is to feel the emotions that we have avoided.

> *I think the habit of maintaining negative thought forms is supported in our culture.* It is more acceptable in our society to have negative thoughts about people and to malign them behind their back, than it is to express negative emotions to their face. We don't have an appropriate model in which to do this. It would be much more appropriate to look inside and find the negative emotions we have towards ourselves. Usually, we have negative feeling toward another because interacting with that person evokes some sort of negative feeling toward the self.
> (Brennan, 1993)

As Brennan so eloquently states, repressed emotions and negative thoughts have significant impacts on our mental and physical well-being, and yet we live in a culture that appears to encourage the continual blocking of negative emotions and thoughts about ourselves, preventing them from being felt or spoken.

Unfortunately, many people habitually repress their emotions and continue to express ongoing moral judgements in stories about themselves and the world; this habit serves only to limit their access to the flow of a natural and more authentic way of being.

The purpose of this book is twofold: first, to explore how our judgemental minds create mental thought "k(not)s" or stories that act to limit our access to the flow of natural joy and acceptance; and second, to provide approaches that allow the release of these mental k(not)s in order to live an authentic life that realises our true potential.

CHAPTER 1

The Judgemental K(not)s that Limit the Flow

When we experience judgemental thoughts, they indicate that some aspects of our current situation are not in accordance with our authentic flow of energy and natural ease. In particular, the brain—or specifically, our thinking—is the origin of these stories. I'll explore a type of cultural mentality I call "blame-game programming" and show how it assists in depressing and repressing our emotions through the reinforcement of judgemental thoughts that locate blame on someone (yourself or others). I call these sophisticated mental stories about events and/or people "k(not)s."

These stories are like recorded responses that replay in our minds, telling us that certain people, events, or even our own behaviours are reasons we're not happy. Have you noticed patterns in the stories that keep coming up in your mind? In this chapter, we're going to explore the link between our thinking, our perceptions of the world, and the way the world may actually exist.

Please read the following statements and ask if you've ever said them to yourself (perhaps with slightly different wording) and if you believe that they are true: My life (or aspects of my world) should not be like this. I am not powerful enough to create my life the way I choose. I cannot trust my world, and so I must control it.

I used to believe that all of these statements were true to varying degrees, although I didn't realise it until I was in my mid-forties. When I came to this realization, I began to wonder why I thought this way and how I'd come to believe in these three key assumptions about life so strongly. I now realise that I grew up in a culture that reinforces the belief that the world is a limited place where the lucky few have access to more than enough and the majority must struggle to get a share of what's left. And if we don't get our fair share, then it's someone's fault! I call this cultural mindset "blame-game" mental programming, because it is based upon a judgemental view that seeks to place blame on someone or something for what appears to be wrong in our lives. A blame-game culture is characterised by a viewpoint that if life is not working out the way we want it to, then there is wrongness in the world, and we seek to locate where the blame is to be placed.

At first glance, the world view we have developed appears to be our normal reality; therefore, we are prone to feeling uncomfortable when confronted with the idea that our so-called reality is actually a cultural construct. Indeed, the way we think about the world is so ingrained in our perceptions that we believe our construct represents the world as it actually exists. In fact, it may not be possible to agree on an objective reality, as we will discuss in later chapters.

Notice how our newspapers, radio, and television programs tell us who is to blame on a regular basis and how many of our conversations focus on our judgements about particular people or situations. In fact, we often align ourselves with other people primarily because we share a similar view of the world with them; this is a tribal view that says we feel most comfortable with those who agree with our judgements.

How does blame-game programming limit our beliefs and therefore restrict our authenticity? This is a subtle issue that I will explain in more depth throughout the book, but essentially, it creates a sense of limitation within ourselves—in that we are not enough and lack in one way or another—and therefore we must seek ways to increase our sense of power and worth. My parents raised me in an environment that supported this blame-game view; everything—including love—was anything but abundant. Rather, it was limited.

To have a part of the American pie (yes, I'm American by birth), I needed to do the right thing and be judged as worthy. If I didn't feel worthy, there had to be a cause to blame: myself, my family, or perhaps even my world in its entirety. I struggled with feeling that I wasn't good enough for many years. I tried to find the job, partner, or lifestyle that would allow me to feel loved and accepted. Somehow I just couldn't feel loved even when I did have a partner or feel worthy even when I did have a job. What prevented me from really knowing that I was fine just as I was? And did others feel the same way, or was it just me who was somehow insufficient and insecure?

I had a breakdown before I had the breakthrough that would save my life. Afterwards, I started to piece together the evidence and work out why my world had shattered so violently. The answer that I eventually came up with was shocking. It was my thinking; it had entirely shaped the way I felt about my life. It was not a consequence of difficult early experiences within my family, my health, my university education or being born as a white woman in a Western culture. All of these did contribute to the mental view I had built up about the world, but at the heart of it all, there was a fundamental, core world view that secretly shaped how I saw myself and my relationship with the world.

The blame-game cultural program that I uncovered in my thinking process reinforced pernicious stories in my mind. It functions by making out that objects outside of us or our own innate deficiencies block the flow of love, joy, and abundance. This type of thought program or pattern of thinking creates a distinctive way for us to view ourselves; it dictates how we speak to one another, how we act in the world, and even what we expect from the world around us. The program is so intrinsically woven into our lives that we can't easily separate ourselves from it. Because blame-game mental programming limits who we think we are, it keeps us living in fear through the application of our judgemental stories.

Another way to view the three statements is as *k(not)s:* "My life is *not* . . . because . . ." "I am *not* . . . because . . ." "The world is *not* . . . because . . ."

We often say these words to ourselves or out loud to others. Do we realise how many times a day we say such things—hundreds, perhaps? I call these kinds of statements "blame-game k(not)s," because when we judge ourselves, other people, or the world, we operate from a blame-game view. That view ties our natural connections to the flow of our authentic beings in knots. We literally reverse the flow when we say words that limit who we are and what the world is; rather than confirming our unlimited potential, we block it.

Judgement, in terms of our thoughts, speech, and actions, is a major block to being authentic. But don't we require judgement to function as human beings in a complex society?

Judgement can be one of two kinds: *moralising judgements,* by which we assert that the label we attach to an object (including the self) is true (for example, the kind of judgement that labels people and things as good or bad); and *discerning judgements,* by which we assess a person, an object, or even ourselves as being (or not being) in harmony with our values. The difference may seem subtle. However, it is similar to knowing when and how to use a knife—it is not the knife that is harmful or beneficial but our application of it. The same is true with judgement; we tend to overuse it to the point of harming others and particularly ourselves, and that is especially the case with moralising judgement.

"Should not" and "should" thoughts also create moralising judgements. We use these words to tell ourselves that someone ought to comply with the patterns of behaviour that we approve of, and if they don't, we condemn them as bad, evil, or misguided. Yet our label, whatever it is, is simply a projection of what we believe is wrong. Wrongness doesn't actually occur in anything or anyone *per se.* It occurs in our perceptions. However, judgement is so common in Western thinking that we don't question it. Next time you're having a conversation, notice how often you or others make statements about something you don't like in society, in someone else, or in yourself.

What purpose does moralising judgement have for us as individuals? It clearly defines us as opposed to "them"— whether it is the self and another person or our clan and another clan. It always places one in a superior position and the other as less superior. In tribal cultures, this enables tribes to maintain their cultural stability so that individuals do not seek outside knowledge or attempt to think or act outside of the defined limits of accepted behavioural norms. It creates strong tribal loyalties and a sense of safety, whether the groups are families, employees, sporting teams, religious groups, or any other type of identity with a demographic, cultural, or ideological characteristic. Judgement allows us to maintain a sense of boundaries about what we believe is right or wrong, and it maintains our own sense of boundedness within a limited range of social behaviours.

Judgement itself is not a problem. Discerning judgement can inform us that we may need to alter our behaviours, either quickly in response to a current situation or in the longer term to reassess our strategy. We do so in order to remain part of the tribe or just to live our values more fully. Yet we now live in an increasingly interdependent society where cooperation is central to our need not just for survival, but also to become authentic and self-fulfilled individuals. If too much judgement separates us and creates unhealthy thought processes, then how do we effectively use judgement to help us maintain the flow of an authentic life?

The key lies in the *balanced* use of judgement so that we remain aware while not underreacting or overreacting to situations. Judgement is a thought process; yet, as mentioned earlier, emotions are helpful in making clear and sound decisions. However, our emotions can also hinder the use of judgement, because we're often not accustomed to the energetic aspect of emotions. A judgement associated with a strong emotion can often be difficult to manage, as we can react to a situation based on prior experiences rather than a real, momentary threat.

Imagine if you were a four-year-old girl wearing a yellow dress, and you went outside to play. A neighborhood boy then ran up to you and shouted "ugly dress," and then you thought to yourself, "I should not have put on this dress," and ran back inside the house feeling miserable. You then unconsciously decided to dislike the color yellow and avoid clothes with that color in the future. Now, as an adult, you still avoid the color but can't remember why you don't like it.

If someone buys you a yellow top, you immediately feel bad and perhaps even label that person as unthoughtful.

The overuse of moralising judgement occurs when we unconsciously associate a negative emotion with an object, person, or aspect of ourselves, which is then avoided, negated, or labeled as bad into the future. The stories we create around prior experiences allow us to label the world with categories that shape our responses and let us feel safe. Blame-game programming happens early in life as we start labeling experiences and people, and then these labels become our templates for how we feel about life in general. The degree to which our thoughts are controlled by this programming depends upon how much we have been exposed to a culture and family that spoke and acted from its particular perspective. Of course, we are also influenced by our unique biological and psychological self-development and the extent to which we believe in the stories that our minds create.

When we react emotionally to events or the possibility of future events, it can often be due to feelings emerging from a prior experience, rather than from an actual threat. The key message in releasing blame-game thinking is that that we're not actually seeing the situation as it is, but rather as our mental programming directs us to "see," as shown in Figure 1.

The judgemental k(not)s that are created are not easily recognised, as we have been operating by their rules for most of our lives. However, we can overcome our unconscious thinking with effort, and when we do, we will unlock access to our true potential. It takes repeated practice to allow feelings to arise without the story running full speed ahead. There are many practices and approaches that can assist us in waking up from the judgemental stories that we tell ourselves. Once we use them, we will find ourselves living in the moment rather than the past or future. With persistence, we will be able to move through the story back to our original emotions and then let go of the judgements that prevent our flow of authentic being.

Original event
▼
Emotions and thoughts occur in relation to event
▼
A moralising judgement about the emotion creates a story
▼
Emotion not fully expressed, and therefore suppressed
▼
Block in flow of life energy and ease
▼
Current event raises similar emotion
▼
Story and moralising judgement arises
▼
Continued emotional suppression
▼
Increased tension and blocking of flow
▼
Leads to depression and/or anxiety and/or aggression

Figure 1. The blame-game cultural programming process that occurs within an individual.

The remainder of this book provides guidance in releasing our blame-game programming (beliefs). What is called reality is far more malleable than we ever imagined, and so are our beliefs! And when we align ourselves with our authentic self by letting our natural emotions flow and releasing the judgemental stories that limit our true abundance, then our lives will be full of ease and joy rather than struggle and poverty.

This book is not simply about positive thinking and manifestation, as affirmations will not manifest if we continue to harbour subconscious negative feelings about ourselves. It is not enough to simply believe what is written here; you have to discover if it's true for you. If you find it has some value, then try experimenting with larger aspects of your life story, your goals, and even your own identity. Are you really who you think you are?

A blame-game mind says that you are a limited being, with limited resources, living in a limited world. This is simply a thought program that you were given early in life. Maybe you only received part of the programming, but I'll bet that you've still got some left. Therefore, this book will be of value to you.

The following chapters are structured as lessons on how to untie each major k(not) in the blame-game program. First, the k(not) is explained, and then certain approaches are presented for releasing thoughts and allowing the repressed emotions to be expressed in a safe way. At the end of each chapter is a series of practices that focus on the lessons given for untying that k(not). The more you focus on the new thoughts and allow the natural expression of your feelings, the stronger your capacity to untie each k(not) will be.

Often, when we begin living more fully in the flow of authentic being, we are likely to experience the deepest aspects of our own versions of the blame-game mind popping up with a message that screams, "This is scary, and we should k(not) be doing, being, saying, etc." Then we close down again, because our programming has told us to. Therefore, living as our authentic selves takes some patience and downright sweat and tears for us to realise our full potential.

If you yearn to experience an authentic life, then spend time letting yourself *feel* and see what your intuition tells you is necessary for getting what you really deserve (and doing it legally). Search for answers in everyday life, and ask for guidance. You will eventually receive all the answers, although they might show up in unlikely places. Be aware, and be brave.

CHAPTER 2

Key 1 – Reset

Move from Rejection to Acceptance of Your Emotions and Experiences

Have you noticed how much of our experiences we reject? Our minds decide what we like and dislike on an ongoing basis with a constant stream of "this is good" and "that is bad" being recorded in our brains. We often believe the content of this incessant chatter to the point of forming entire belief systems based upon the (judgemental) stories that we create in our minds. As explained in chapter 1, this type of moralising judgement can repress our emotions, which in turn, leads to our creating mental stories in relation to ourselves and our lives, and these block our natural flow of authenticity.

The feeling that "I should k(not) be experiencing this" is a subtle one, often occurring at a very deep level. It is derived from a type of story that suggests that we are somehow deficient, that a particular situation is not right, or that something will get worse. If we have ever experienced serious trauma, then we have even deeper fears about the future, as we don't want to re-experience that particular event again. There are perfectly good reasons for our mental wiring wanting us to avoid certain situations, as they might, potentially, be dangerous. Children learn not to touch the stove burner after scorching their fingers just once!

As indicated earlier, there is a knife-edge difference between using our *discerning* judgement to guard against real danger so as to act appropriately and believing in our *moralising* judgemental story, which seduces us into avoiding our feelings about an event or a person. When we judge an event or person as causing a negative feeling in us, we are choosing to disown the feelings in ourselves that we find difficult to accept.

Therefore, when we reject experiences or people, we are rejecting emotional experiences inside ourselves that are actually seeking to be expressed. Because our society is generally uncomfortable with the expression of feelings, it is acceptable to transmute those feelings into a "blame" thought. Often we might verbalise these thoughts later to another person who is not connected to the original event or simply blame ourselves and maintain an internal mental story.

This process all seems so natural because we're immersed in the culture of blame-game thoughts from an early age! However, it is simply a type of mental programming and not natural at all. It is not in accordance with our authentic nature, and this is why we experience an ongoing low level of anxiety. The blame-game thoughts are in conflict with our natural state of ease through emotional release that we are unconsciously seeking.

Therefore, to begin unravelling this programming requires us to first allow and accept our thoughts and experiences. If we begin by rejecting the blame-game thoughts, we haven't changed the game at all. We want to change the rules of the game, and the first rule is to accept. To accept is simply to know that what is happening is reality. If we feel scared, then we accept this feeling. If we are in physical pain, we accept the sensations in our bodies and try to connect more fully with them in an emotional sense as well.

For example, you may be experiencing the pain of a toothache. Yet, you may emotionally resist the pain, as it means you need to go to the dentist and you have often felt anxiety about going. By fully allowing the pain, which doesn't mean you can't take some type of pain relief, you begin to then contact the underlying emotional story of not wanting to see the dentist. This story is simply a fear that wants some attention, and by letting yourself hear and feel the story, you can reveal what it is actually about. Perhaps you felt embarrassed the last time you visited the dentist, because you accidentally almost bit down on his fingers! By giving yourself some empathy around this fear, the pain in the present moment may actually feel less strong and less threatening.

Acceptance is therefore engaging with the senses of our entire being—relaxing into what is happening, mentally, physically, and emotionally. Again, this doesn't mean we are controlling our thoughts and feelings. Rather, we are observers engaged in contemplating the activity, yet not caught up in the thoughts that label it either good or bad.

As we accept what is arising within us, we simply notice the judgemental stories that may be present. When we observe these stories without becoming entangled in them, they often begin to dissipate because they no longer have the emotional fuel to keep running down the normal track. At that point, we can allow any natural emotions to arise and be safely expressed. Often these emotions relate to present or past needs that are demanding our attention. If we choose to express or act on these needs, then we can notice a shift towards relief when we authentically speak or take action. The final step is letting go of the possibility that our needs will be met exactly as we want them to be met. This process is illustrated in Figure 2.

In the following chapters, I provide examples of how to move through each of the steps in the process of releasing blame-game programming and allowing your authentic being to shine through. This can be a quite gradual process, as we are unlearning past thought-programs that we strongly identify with and thus rewiring our bodies and brains to a different way of being. The key is to notice the emotional tension whenever it arises and to allow its unfolding without trying to fix or change it.

Original event
▼
Emotions and thoughts occur in relation to event
▼
Acceptance of emotions and thoughts
▼
Judgemental story released
▼
Emotions fully and safely expressed
▼
Empathise with current needs/values
▼
Act with dignity; release control
▼
Flow of authentic being continues

Figure 2. The flow of authentic being.

When we begin to allow life to be as it is, then the connection to our authentic beings starts to flow more easily and we feel more at ease and more joyful. This doesn't mean we automatically begin to feel more trusting, happy, etc. right away! That feeling might appear, then it may disappear for a while, so be patient as we are resetting our programming. This is not a linear process.

You Have to Feel to Heal

A blame-game program runs on the emotion of fear. Because fear is so commonly felt, we often don't realise how much of our own lives are driven by trying to not feel fear, to avoid fear, or to placate fear! Fear is a projection of our beliefs into future scenarios—whether in seconds, minutes, or years.

What we often fear the most is the act of facing up to our own vulnerabilities. Many of us would rather be physically harmed than have to confront our inner emotions regarding how we feel about ourselves. Why is emotional pain so feared? Probably because we don't know what to do with it; it's like a stranger who knocks on the door, and you don't want to answer because you don't know what he might do!

In actuality, that stranger at the door is your friend. He has come to bring you a message. Indeed, all emotions are messengers, and there is nothing to fear in either the message or the messenger. We have simply become conditioned to believe that we should k(not) become too emotional, as that is not conducive to being a rational individual.

The Sufi poet, Rumi, beautifully describes the movement of emotions in his poem "The Guest House."

This being human is a guest house.
Every morning a new arrival.
A joy, a depression, a meanness,
Some momentary awareness comes
as an unexpected visitor.

Welcome and entertain them all!
Even if they're a crowd of sorrows,
who violently sweep your house
empty of its furniture,
still, treat each guest honourably.

He may be clearing you out
for some new delight.

The dark thought, the shame, the malice,
meet them at the door laughing,
and invite them in.

Be grateful for whoever comes,
because each has been sent
as a guide from beyond.
(Barks, 2004)

Of course, if we are having strong emotions—for example, feeling incredibly angry at someone—then we often need to find ways to release these emotions safely. However, anger itself is not a problem, and neither is any other emotion. The issue is how to responsibly release the energy associated with the emotion. When we take responsibility for our emotions and learn how to appreciate the messages that they hold, then it is easier for us to release that energy in positive ways. We'll explore this idea more in the next chapter.

The word *emotion* actually gives us a clue as to its function: to be "in motion." If we allow an emotion to move freely without attempting to suppress it, then it may not be as strong as it seemed, and it will simply release energy easily. Alternatively, when we hold on tightly to an emotion, then the energy builds up and it can later feel like it may explode within us.

The main issue that confronts us in this modern world in relation to emotional expression is that we generally don't learn from our families or our cultures how to express the full range of emotions without causing harm to ourselves or other people. There may exist some families and even communities who do understand how to allow emotions to be released naturally, yet this seems to be quite rare in the Western world.

Personally, I did not know how to do this as a young child—or even know that there was an alternative way besides repression. I knew that I didn't feel comfortable with emotions and was even somewhat fearful of them! Later in my adult life, I learned that we can release emotions as they occur without making negative judgements upon ourselves or upon the people who we believe caused the feelings to occur.

Emotions are simply energetic signals in our psychological and physical being. Essentially, they can originate as a simple response to an event—often without our awareness of any precursor thought. More commonly, emotions arise from a thought. The emotion we experience is an indicator of how our thought does (or does not) align with what our mental programs dictate is appropriate. This inner model is made up of a combination of values, beliefs, experiences, and knowledge about how we see ourselves in relation to the physical and nonphysical world. I use the term nonphysical to denote the mental, emotional, and spiritual aspects of our existence, although they are inter-related with our physical being.

Let's explore the idea that emotions are indicators of the degree of fit between our realities and our mental programs about ourselves and the world. For example, your dog dies, and you feel sad. But what is it that makes you feel sad? It is actually the loss of connection and friendship that you enjoyed that you feel sad about—something positive that occurred in your life that is now gone.

So, we can see that emotions are primarily about our current mental programming, which is to a large degree focused on ourselves. In the case of your dog dying, you may actually have a mix of emotions. For instance, if he were hit by a car, then you would regret that you didn't fix the hole in the fence. So, the first thought that would arise is: "I'm responsible for his death, because I should have fixed that fence." At first, you may feel angry at yourself, and then you may think about how much you miss him. You would be sad, and these emotions would alternate, producing a mixture of guilt and slight depression. We would have a hard time accepting the situation as it now exists.

Such a feeling will be prolonged and even deepened if we have a difficult time accepting that the event happened (or is happening). We will continue to think badly about ourselves, and that will increase the guilty feeling. Why do we have such a hard time letting ourselves off the hook?

First, we often don't really know how to be sad and let out the deep emotions. There are two scenarios that could be occurring in our unconscious minds to keep the k(not) in place. It could be that our reactions are linked to past events where we felt a similar guilt; therefore, it's rising to the surface more strongly than we'd expect in relation to that one event. Alternatively, there could be another aspect of our lives where we currently have unexpressed emotions (which we haven't acknowledged), and this has triggered a wave of feeling that seems unexplained, yet we sense there is something underlying it.

An inability to adequately feel emotions and allow them to come to the surface naturally as they arise is a block to releasing our judgemental thoughts. The thought continues to block the emotion, and the emotion becomes stronger. Further, we become transfixed with our thoughts and often don't even question the story that arises with them.

The first step in connecting back with our authentic being is to sense the emotions that are present and then attempt to feel them, even if we're not consciously able to give them names. Emotions are messengers, and they can help us identify our unexpressed pain in relation to past or present events—or both.

Learning to feel begins with becoming more aware of the sensations in our bodies. Where does the emotion seem to reside? When I'm angry, it often starts as tightness in my throat or jaw. Where is it for you? If you're happy, does your body feel relaxed? If not, see if you can identify a tension somewhere or perhaps just a sensory numbness.

Meditation is one of the most beneficial ways of connecting more fully with our bodies and our emotions, especially if done in a way that allows those emotions to be completely experienced. It is possible to develop a detachment from emotions if we simply experience the bodily sensation and then don't allow the connected feeling to be expressed, which may serve to maintain the repressed emotions. Vipassana meditation is excellent in developing awareness of the body and even of thoughts. However, for meditation to be effective in creating a link from story to emotion, there needs to be a focus on the sensation in the body of sufficient duration for the meditator to get in touch with the emotion. A meditation technique called focusing is a helpful approach.

In summary, the first steps in accessing our authentic selves are allowing feelings to exist, and then noticing their content (if they are sad, angry, fearful, and so on) without becoming lost in them or trying to suppress them. In the following sections, we'll explore ways to nurture and be kind to our feelings, as they are really a very important aspect of our capacity to connect to an authentic way of being.

You have to feel to heal means that emotions are your dashboard indicators of well-being, and the more you pay attention to them, the easier it is to express your authentic self.

An Empathic Welcome Mat

I learned about the practice of self-empathy not so long ago, and I have since found it to be the most amazing tool for self-healing. If you're experiencing an emotional or physical issue, consulting with psychologists, counsellors, healers, and doctors to assist with your healing may be important. Yet, the results I've seen when I simply listen to my own authentic being have led me to believe absolutely in our innate capacity to heal ourselves.

When I say, "I listen to my authentic being," what exactly am I talking about? Let me explain. Once we have let go of our judgemental stories, then it is easier to hear our still voices within. I begin by focusing my attention on my body and noticing what is arising there. Then, I ask, "What's happening?" as I would to a dear friend. Finally, I just allow whatever is occurring in my body and mind to simply happen by dropping any resistance I might have to it at that moment. In the relaxed state that follows, I often have quiet thoughts emerge that otherwise could not break through the walls of my normal chattering mind.

Self-empathy is the act of listening to our quiet, authentic selves. It is the single most important practice that I would recommend to anyone who desires to really shift their world and connect with a more authentic and meaningful life. Why? Because most of us are likely to be in a deficit of empathy—our empathy tanks have been running on low for years, and we are constantly searching for someone to fill it. We secretly hope that other people will take care of us and thus fill the black hole that seems to be constantly sucking out our life energies. Perhaps I'm being a bit dramatic, but seriously, all too often we look outside of ourselves for the very thing we can be giving ourselves from within!

Once we start practicing self-empathy, it's not long before we realise how hard we've been on ourselves throughout life. Please, try not to feel too bad about this, as it's simply our blame-game programming that has been repeating itself over and over again, like a stuck tape deck (sorry—iPod for the younger folks). In fact, it becomes downright astonishing to begin noticing our inner critics that are constantly berating us, judging us, and comparing us with others. When I started self-empathy practice, I couldn't believe how critical I'd been of myself and continued to be, although with reduced frequency.

My theory about why people engage in the distractions of overwork, drugs, television, partying, alcohol, and excessive entertainment or sports is that they can't handle being alone with their own thoughts and emotions. When alone, we are forced to deal with the barrage of our negative programming, which may range from dull to outright brutal.

I was a workaholic for the first twenty years of my adult life, and in retrospect, it is easy for me to acknowledge that I was avoiding listening to my real feelings and thoughts.

A regular quiet time is very conducive to going beyond the mind's usual mental ramblings. It can be a bit scary once you start tuning into your whole being more closely. You're so used to believing that the constant play of words in your head is "you" that often the clear and subtle inner voice, which is your authentic being, cannot be heard.

When we begin giving ourselves the time to slow down and engage with our feelings more directly, then it is useful to have a good friend or trusted counsellor nearby. Because we are now becoming open to our emotions, they might burst out suddenly, and it is comforting to be able to sit with a friend who is empathetic and has a big stack of tissues. No one is capable of handling her own stuff all the time—we all need a sense of shared support, and it is insane to try to handle everything ourselves.

We can also use the handy empathy mat when we're faced with difficult situations and unsure of what actions to take. It is like having a pause button on our brains and mouths that suspends judgement about a particular event until we have checked in with ourselves more fully. We might ask ourselves how we really feel about it. Is there more that we need to explore before reacting or making a decision? If you find yourself in a situation and realise that you don't want to respond right away, then it is perfectly reasonable to request that you take a few minutes (or hours) to collect your thoughts before choosing what to say or do next.

Remember that the empathy mat is always available— 24/7—and that it can help you with any issue, no matter how significant. Try it out a few times each day and see what a difference it can make in your life. Then, when you start getting really skilled at tuning into your own feelings and thoughts, try putting a mat out for someone else. That is a genuine gift that will give deeply to you both.

———————◁●▷———————

An empathetic welcome mat is about being a kind friend to yourself. It is the simplest and most effective means of connecting to your inner authentic self.

———————◁●▷———————

Call Off the Search Party

Have you been waiting for something to happen before your life really takes off? Are you in constant search mode? Do you often say to yourself: "I do not yet have the perfect partner, the perfect job, or the perfect me!" If only they (or you) would meet your expectations, then life would be so good!

So much of our lives seem to be spent in search mode, either waiting for perfection or being disappointed when events, people, and even our own behaviours don't match up to the dreams we have created in our minds.

But, what if life were delivering exactly what we ordered? Perhaps we didn't have such perfect dreams after all. What if the fantasy partner was a projection of our concepts, but we hadn't realised what our ideal partner really meant. Let's say we've decided upon an easy-going kind of person as a partner, and we meet someone who initially seems to fit this description. Yet, after a few months of spending time with that person, we find their lack of initiative and motivation unbearably boring, as they are so relaxed about everything.

An ongoing dissatisfaction with some aspect of ourselves and/or our lives is again a type of judgement about what we, or others, should or should not be, have, or say. We are continually searching for the next best thing and believe that if we found it, then somehow our lives would be different and, of course, better than it is at present.

The holy grail of finding "it" (as well as getting rid of it) can occupy much of our time. The feeling of wanting something else can be pervasive, or it may only be occasional and fleeting. However, we often have our own patterns of dissatisfaction, being happy with some aspect of our lives but not with some other part. For example, I'm generally quite content with my weight and appearance and my circle of close friends (even as some change over time). However, I struggled with finding a life partner for many years, and I still have eruptions of unhappiness that can create havoc in my relationship with my current partner.

This obsession with finding the perfect elements that are supposed to bring us happiness can be destructive in more ways than one. It can prevent us from appreciating what we have right now, and it can also prevent us from seeing the inner judgements that we carry around about the world.

I have discovered that if we aren't satisfied with our lives, then there are only two solutions:

1. Change our judgemental blame-game programming and life habits.
2. Change our programming and life habits while also changing our circumstances.

I know it is difficult to accept, but this is actually the reality of our world. We often do need to get a new career, dump the sloth-like boyfriend, or move to Transylvania. However, these physical actions alone will never really change our world. A new sloth-like boyfriend will show up in Transylvania, and we'll wonder how this keeps on happening to us.

A major insight that I have had in my own life is that events are not neutral—I interpret them in a particular way according to my judgemental stories. The theory of neutral events is interesting for several reasons. First, although it is easy to regard events either as culturally appropriate or not, this is still a judgement on our part. But if we look more deeply into our own judgement of events and people, we can see that our world view is a story that is unique to us, and just because we have come to believe in our stories does not necessarily make them true. Finally, as we think, so we are, and as we think about the world, so it is.

Our perceptions about the way the world works is actually better thought of as a working theory. We're taught to judge particular actions and events without first understanding why judgement could potentially limit what our own perceptions tell us. Recently, the magazine *New Scientist* featured a special issue titled "What is Reality?" (Brooks 2012). It contained interviews with leading physicists seeking to understand how our consciousness influences the reality that we observe. Although there is disagreement and speculation about particular aspects of how reality is observed by our consciousness, there is increasing agreement that our individual consciousness actually creates the reality that we believe is neutral.

If our conscious minds are capable of shaping the reality we see and feel, then how does this occur? My hypothesis, based upon my experience and from many sources of literature, is that our thoughts and emotions are energy. Because everything that exists in the world is energy as well, then our thoughts and emotions can attract people and events, and this mostly happens on a subconscious level.

Throughout the book, I'll try to explain further how our thoughts and the external world are linked, but in a reverse way to our normal perceptions. That is, our thinking actually has a role in co-creating how the world appears to us.

If we start at the most fundamental level of our mental programming, where our thoughts originate, then there are only two choices for each thought. It can carry an emotion of *fear* (blame game) or of *love* (authentic). So, each thought we have can then signal to our bodies and then move outward into the world that we are either fearful or loving. Almost everyone has a mixture; therefore, the way we view the world will also be a mixture.

To begin moving towards thinking more loving thoughts is to question those sneaky, almost unconscious, thoughts that elicit greater fear in us, especially those preceding our emotions. Our blame-game judgemental program says to us that when something feels bad, then either we're bad or the object out there is bad. It doesn't give us a choice, because often the story has already begun to play out, and it directs us as to who or what is the problem. Often, the program will direct us to simply avoid or eliminate the problem and start searching again for perfection. It is as though we have a covert spy that keeps whispering "the problem is there or there," and then we go looking for it and blame that thing for what seems wrong in our lives. The spy is our thoughts, and it prevents us from fully feeling and also understanding the deeper program that is playing, which keeps us in a state of fear.

Fear is fuelled by an inner state of consciousness that relies upon a thought story to inform us of what is happening out there through judgement of people and events. When we're fearful, our basic instinct at a physiological level is either fight or flight. We either confront or avoid the person, and the same goes for the situation. Yet, our fear is actually based on a series of judgements made prior to the event in question. Can we be fearful of something we've never encountered before? Probably not, unless we relate it to something that we have previously encountered and thus already know. So, it is our prior judgemental stories that inform us as to the appropriateness of our responses to our current situations.

When we act or react from a sense of fear, this may lead to further judgement and an increased searching for something else that will give us comfort. It is actually our minds that are seeking rest from the constant intrusion of one damn fearful thing after another. Judgement gives us a way out of that fear, at least for a moment, although it is a false sense of security because the mind is still fearful of that object even though it has been temporarily vanquished.

Calling off the search party is about realising that we have been lured into our own stories again. Our thoughts have developed an absolute power over us so that we act as if every story they tell is true. Most of our thoughts are from our programming; therefore, we should view much of what we think with suspicion.

To change the storylines, we must first catch ourselves in the stories and notice the patterns in our thoughts and in our lives. In which parts of our lives do we find it difficult to have harmony or contentment? What do our stories tell us, and can we allow ourselves to listen to what lies under the judgement? What deeper feelings are present, and can we connect to them rather than quickly pushing them aside?

We are particularly preoccupied with searching for another time other than *right now*. See if you can catch yourself in that search mode. Are you daydreaming about a future moment or, on the other hand, becoming entangled in a past event?

Why is the present moment so slippery that we can't stay present? It's because we do not really trust ourselves or this world, and we want to escape from our immediate feelings and thoughts. To be with our pain or whatever we're experiencing is to stop judging life, others, and especially ourselves. Does that mean passivity? No, it means the absolute opposite. We can make clearer choices and take action when we are fully present, responding to the events of this direct moment and observing our reactions to it.

To call off the search party is to accept the present moment and to acknowledge your contribution to the situation. If you desire change, then become aware that your thought patterns and emotions are informing you of what changes are needed internally in order to influence the reality of your life.

Accender

You're right; the word *accender* is not in the dictionary. Its intention is to create an enigma for our minds, similar to one of those Zen koan sayings that you've always thought were somewhat silly, like, "What is the sound of one hand clapping?"

Accender is a two-step dance that we can learn in order to stop looking like freaks on the dance floor of life. Have you noticed how we often behave in totally bizarre ways, appearing to be contradictory or unpredictable to others and even to ourselves? This occurs because we act from fear rather than love and because we haven't properly understood how our own thinking influences what we see as our realities. In learning to dance in a more graceful way with life, we start to flow more with its movement rather than trying to predict every note ahead of time or to blame the music for our missteps.

For example, a woman might be interested in younger men, and then she dates a man ten years younger. (Let's say she's fifty.) The man doesn't meet her expectations, so her story is that "younger men are too dull." Is it actually appropriate to determine all future life experiences based on just one incident? That's often what is done by our judgemental minds: labelling something as bad, unsupportive, and problematic simply on the basis of one life event.

Now, it may be true that we have experienced some difficult circumstances in our lives and that we want to avoid similar ones in the future. That's what is called *discerning judgement*. If, however, we begin to label in some way every potential person or event that remotely resembles a particular difficult experience, then we set up a *moral judgement* about it. Such moralising is actually an act of fear, which reinforces our stories about the world, based as they are on limited experience.

To dance with life is therefore to not become transfixed on either what we see as bad or as good, and that includes external situations, people, and, ultimately, ourselves. To move with the flow of an authentic life and not become too engrossed in appearances, it's important that we learn accender. Here's how it goes.

The first step is with our left foot. Left is generally regarded as the artsy side—it likes incomprehensible concepts such as love, beauty, truth, and the meaning of blue fruit.

You move the left foot with trust and grace as it steps wholly into a pile of dog shit. I mean the real stuff—fresh and steaming, maybe even with bits of unidentifiable plastic or . . . well, you get the idea.

So, hence, the first move is to *accept.*

Thus, it's good to start visualising the poo right off, because we all know it's easy to accept nice things like stepping into freshly cut grass or onto a lovely silk rug. But, when suddenly it finds contact with soft, smelly, oh-so-disgusting poo, the reaction is to *reject* this experience. *Get that poo off my foot as soon as possible!*

Accepting is not like saying it's just wonderful that doggie poo is slathered on my foot. No, it's just looking at the stuff and seeing it for itself. A sense of curiosity about it arises at the same time that we know that it isn't a big deal. If we want to say rude things about the poo, we do so but then just wipe it off and go on with dancing again.

The second step is with the right foot. (See how natural this is?) The right side is more aligned with practical things like knowing to fill up with fuel before the fuel gauge hits empty.

Because the left foot has already stepped into the poo, the right one might be a bit more cautious and concerned; therefore, it will begin telling me to put on some shoes. Then, a whole train of thought (a story) will begin putting down its tracks in my head: "I should not be walking on this grass without shoes. And I should not take this path, as it might have more poo."

You know how this train goes . . . . The right foot is so concerned with doggie-doo that it cannot enjoy the luscious cut grass lying seductively in its path. It starts getting tied up in *k(not)s*—about what should not be done and what should not happen.

Therefore, the second move is to *surrender.*

Surrender to the possibility of green grass or of more dog poo. Either may come to pass in the future—who can say? Of course, we can look out for both but not become obsessive in either case.

This means parking our strong desire to have or not have something happen. We can use common sense, and if a large Great Dane is squatting ahead, then steer clear! Perhaps we can even be curious to see if more poo happens and then just allow our reactions to occur but do nothing except observe ourselves and the poo.

Why is accender important for our well-being? Because, as creatures of comfort, we like knowing what is ahead of us—literally in space and, chronologically, in our future. This means we want to know that we can continue to have more of the stuff we like and less of the experiences we don't like. Yet, in our physical world, what happens around us is not that predictable (or not in the way we believe it to be). Therefore, it is not that we should try to shape the world to our preferences but rather that we might endeavour to take a view of life that encompasses the way the world really is. There's a Buddhist saying that sums this up: if we go barefoot and are worried about stones, then we could cover the whole world in leather, or we could instead put leather shoes on our feet.

In our daily lives, we cover up our insecurities by running our stories and judging people and situations to an extreme. Our stories are similar to putting leather over the world so it feels more comfortable to us. What then does wearing leather shoes on our feet mean? I would propose that it is simply accendering to our immediate experience and not taking it too personally. We can begin to gracefully accept and surrender to the unfolding of what each moment brings us.

We feel it as personal simply because it has engaged with an existing story that begins playing, and this elicits a certain feeling in us. Then we confuse the story with the present experience. Wearing the leather is a reminder that we can touch the experience without having to get caught in the pain of the storyline. Stories can also bring us pleasure, and thus we often like to repeat those experiences that reinforce enjoyable feelings. Yet, even such events can bring pain at some point, as no person or experience is purely pleasurable or painful.

When we can accender more easily to ongoing events and even to our own emotions, then the world seems friendlier. The former threats that we envisioned as causing us major problems fade into the background when we start realising that it is not the actual situations causing us emotional pain, but the stories that are playing in our heads.

I know this is a very tricky area to traverse, as I'm still learning myself. I can often become entangled in my own drama, forgetting how subtly and smoothly a story can weave itself into my existing thoughts. Someone once said that we "keep getting surprised by the same damn things." This is exactly the case, as we are often like a fish that gets caught by a fisherman's hook one week and then the next week forgets about the hook and gets caught again!

Check it out for yourself and see what the "same damn thing" is for you. Then, you'll start to catch the tail of the tale, and it will not be as easy for you to get caught next time. This is the way we become conscious of our stories. The next steps are the hardest, because with our increased awareness, we then try to change the habits as they arise—in other words, not act out the stories so strongly.

Accepting the situation as it exists means to remain conscious of our reactions to ensure they don't become extreme. We can probably recognise situations in which we impulsively react again and again. It's exhausting, and yet there is a way out. The spiritual teacher Eckhart Tolle describes this as getting ensnared in our "pain body" (Tolle 2004). I believe the pain he is referring to is emotional pain that arises strongly in reaction to our stories. This pain arises with different flavours—unworthiness, abandonment, loss of self, and, ultimately, death. Tolle suggests bringing our awareness to the present moment and being aware of ourselves as much as we can when such reactions occur. I would add that removing ourselves from the situation may also help us to stay in consciousness—that is, to not allow our stories to run full speed ahead.

Sometimes, if we push ourselves too much and try to overcome our reactions, then it may get worse, as we are using force rather than working with the energy of our emotions. However, maintaining presence by focusing on the emerging feelings and their location in the body can assist us to transform the emotion from one of negativity to neutrality and then to positivity.

An awareness that allows us to more readily accept and surrender to the present moment can be achieved with repeated daily practice in mindfulness. There are numerous forms of meditation, and the most elemental do not require us to be associated with any religious program. The simplest form of meditation is to focus our minds on our breathing, and then, through repeated practice, we gain the capacity to focus when we really need it—when we are under stress!

If we want to keep getting the same results from life as we always have, then we can keep doing the same thing. However, if we desire different results, then it is up to us to try new approaches that allow us to view and respond differently to the same circumstances. Now is actually a great time to start!

Accender means dancing with life: accepting what occurs and what does not occur. It's to step away from personalising every situation and to realise that you can own your reactions, rather than having the reactions own you.

Practices for Chapter 2

Reset: Move from Rejection to Acceptance Our Emotions and Experiences

Practice 1

1. Begin to feel your emotions by welcoming them at all times. Try it now: first feel your heart, sense it beating, and then gently place a small welcome mat in front of it that reads: "I fully accept everything about me right now." Can you notice an immediate sense of relief?

2. Notice what other emotions arise as you continue to allow and accept everything about yourself right now.

This is a powerful practice. So, whenever you notice a feeling of discomfort arising in yourself, no matter how slight, please step onto that mat and say those words of self-empathy.

Practice 2

Write down common judgements you have about:

1. Yourself

2. Your family

3. Your life so far

Take one of those judgements and see if you can feel under the story. What emotions arise in your body and what thoughts in your mind? Try to be impartial about whatever comes up and just observe these thoughts as if you were watching a movie. If emotions arise, then let them come without getting carried away or resisting. Do you notice any themes across the categories? Is there a primary judgement (or story) you seem to be telling yourself?

Practice 3

To practice accender, try doing the following:

1. Write down one event in your life that has been difficult to accept.

2. Then ask "why?"

3. Then look at that answer and ask "why?" again.

4. Do this a third time and maybe even a fourth time.

When you look at that final answer, does it allow any new acceptance for yourself and the situation? Notice how your body feels when it has acceptance as opposed to when it does not. Which way would you rather feel?

CHAPTER 3

Key 2 – Reconnect

Claim Your Authentic Being

As we learn to reset our capacities to feel and express ourselves more authentically, we often become aware that our programming contains limiting thoughts about our lives that are probably not true. I generally categorise any type of thought pattern that sees limitations in our capacity to live more joyful and authentic lives with the statement: "I am not powerful enough to create my life as I choose."

Our minds seek power because it appears as something desirable yet just beyond our reach. We seek the power to create ourselves and our world in the way that we choose—this is the definition of power I'm using in this book.

Although we are attracted to people who appear to be powerful in some way, we intuitively know that power can also be associated with negative thoughts, such as feeling that another person or group has *power over* us physically or mentally. To clarify the concept that someone appears to have power over us requires the differentiation of two kinds of power. The first is internal power, which is generated through positive thoughts and feelings that maintain an ongoing sense that we are co-creators in our lives; the second is external power, which places emphasis on our physical realities as having greater control over our lives, and thus limits our sense of capacity to co-create our life situations. Internal power is the true source of our power in this life.

Our programming tells us to continually search for external ways of getting power, because we have been tricked into believing that it exists outside ourselves. That is, our blame-game programming says that we're not naturally abundant in ourselves; therefore, we must add something onto who we are in order to become powerful.

I grew up believing that I wasn't powerful enough, and so I was constantly looking for ways to make improvements. I even accumulated three university degrees to prove my worth! Of course, I did enjoy the experience of acquiring them and have no regrets. Yet, in retrospect, I know that the feeling of not being enough was an underlying driver.

The belief that you are not enough is a huge k(not) in terms of limiting your belief and capacity for choosing an authentic life. What does "not enough" mean when we feel such limitation within ourselves? I see it as a feeling of not allowing love and acceptance of myself for simply who I am. Being authentic is not about what I own, who I know, or what I do. That last one was a big motivator for me—I used to have a strong belief that I am what I do. My family reinforced the view that what I did for others was the measure of my importance. So, I did as much as I could for other people, even to the detriment of my own health.

Giving to others is obviously good, yet the motivation behind it is critical—do we give from a feeling of love or one of fear? My giving was mixed, and it took me many years to untangle what giving from love really meant and to realise that I could give love abundantly to myself without limiting the amount of it I gave to others. However, being able to say no to others is an important skill in maintaining those boundaries that serve to protect one's well-being.

The thought that "I am not enough" is based on fear developed in early childhood due to a lack of unconditional love from family and society. Most of our cultural conditioning taught us that we must change ourselves in order to be better loved and rewarded. Of course, that is part of the socialisation process that teaches us how to self-reflect on our behaviours in terms of their impacts on others and on ourselves. Yet, when we're young, we easily confuse an adverse judgement of our behaviour by another person with a feeling that we're not "good enough" or not "lovable." Therefore, we begin to feel fear if we don't get approval from others for our behaviours and words, and we go on to form stories around our own inadequacies.

I'm going to now share a story of how I discovered why it is so critical to remove this particular programming k(not) in order to live an authentic life. When I was forty-two, my beautiful older sister, Rachele, committed suicide. Four years later, I spiraled into clinical depression and contemplated taking my own life. Fortunately for me, I maintained a belief that life was actually worth living, although it didn't feel that way at the time. I am eternally grateful that I held on to life by my fingernails. The combination of the two experiences later set in motion a process of inquiry within me to understand why our minds stumble down such dark and lonely paths.

Today, after my own struggle through the black hole of depression, I am now of the view that what killed my sister, and almost destroyed me, was simply a runaway thought program. Let me reframe that: it was the blame-game programming that she received as a young person (and that she continually reinforced throughout her life) that created the beliefs that led to her death.

Some of you might find this shocking, and some may be relieved. I'm not trying to convince anyone that my view is right. It is, however, my deeply felt view, and it is based upon my own first-hand knowledge of depression, as well as my experience as a meditator for more than fifteen years. I have also experienced two years of cognitive behavioural therapy. But I will leave it for you to discover whether I am right.

It might help if I explain further what I mean about being "programmed for depression." My perspective is that Western culture's predominant programming is a blame-game mental thought process that runs on guilt and blame. Notice how many people, you included, accept (at least to some extent) the three primary statements made at the beginning of the book: *this moment is limited, we are limited, and the world is limited*. Again, don't take my word for it. Check it out yourselves—are people mainly complaining about what they don't have, or are they being grateful for what they do have? A complaint culture is one of poverty—and not realising that we can take responsibility for our own needs in an abundant universe.

A blame-game culture creates a process of manipulative jostling for power by whoever can claim the "correct view." Often, this type of competition for power attracts externalisers more than internalisers. People who see the world as defective and insist that they have the right view are externalisers. If bad things happen to them, it's generally somebody else's fault. They take on limited responsibility and, in extreme cases, are sociopaths. Externalisers may also believe that the world is not good enough, even if they are, so there's the glitch in their programming. Conversely, internalisers believe that if bad things happen, then it's their fault. They work harder, do more, and try to be better, even while believing that they're not good enough.

Many individuals have a combination of the externaliser and internaliser program; yet one type usually dominates when the person is under stress. In both cases, the person sees the source of power as being primarily outside of himself (external); therefore, he can easily buy into the blame-game culture. If instead, we embrace the understanding that our definitive source of power is internal, then we release either mode of blaming the world (externalising) or that of blaming ourselves (internalising).

My sister was an internaliser, and she certainly believed she wasn't good enough. She hardly ever asked for help and worked diligently at whatever task she was doing. Someone viewing her from the outside—that is, someone looking at her external self—would have found it difficult to see that she might not value herself. But because her programming said that if something wasn't working well, then it must be her fault, she reasoned that she should do more. Notice the word *do*. It is the key to understanding why depression is caused by a blame-game program. If we aren't good enough, then we must do more. If we really believed we were already good enough, doing more would not be the answer to anything, because we'd be asking the wrong question. It's not a question of asking, "How do we prove we're good enough?" Rather, it's stating, "We are good enough, so there's nothing to prove."

Blame-game programming says we're not enough and our power is limited, creating a view that when life doesn't go our way, it is our fault. That takes us down a deadly spiral into depression. Of course, other factors can increase the likelihood that depression will deepen; they may be physiological (in my case, a lack of iron), emotional (evidenced by trauma or repressed emotions, such as deep sadness), or both. Therefore, I acknowledge that depression has multiple triggers and that it is not simply just about our cultural programming.

However, when we become depressed, we are totally engrossed in our blame-game programming, so much so that it takes over our body-mind almost completely, and our flow is virtually cut off. Our thoughts become incessant, and our bodies and minds cannot seem to find any pleasure in life. If you've ever experienced depression, you'll know how devastating this can be, as the mind sinks further and further into the black hole.

Have you seen the film *The Matrix*? I admire this film's message, because it is completely symbolic of being in or out of blame-game programming. The red pill is the way out, yet it requires us to be courageous and experience some mind-bending realisations and extreme emotions. (Remember how Neo was almost in shock initially after taking the pill?). Therefore, in changing our programming (or even better, eliminating it so there is none), we need to be gentle with ourselves, because we have built our lives so completely around false concepts that are, in reality, mere sand castles.

When we are in blame-game programming, we must continually search for something outside of ourselves to shore up our feelings of inadequacy—hence, the extreme pursuit of money, glamour, sports, food, drugs, or sex. I'm not saying we should abandon all material stuff, but we should simply to begin to ask ourselves if we're searching for something that these items really can't give us. Then, we can start feeling what is happening inside ourselves. What is our story telling us, and is it really true?

The key to getting beyond the story is to allow, feel, and create a new intention that moves us into a *choice* mentality. Stories are like programmed recordings that limit what we believe and restrict how we think and act. First, we each need to catch our own individual story, the one that plays in our minds continually. Next, we need to feel underneath that for the key emotions it produces, and finally, we need to release them.

Setting up an initial intention as, "I am powerful and can create my life as I choose," is the first step in opening up a new dimension to what we commonly conceive as the self. The k(not)s that bind our true natures will unravel and bring us enhanced inner wealth and true peace as we step into new choices about ourselves and our lives.

Embrace Dignity

Do you realise that every one of us is born into royalty? I don't mean that we're all somehow related to Prince Charles, but rather that each human being has an innate worth greater than the riches of all royalty combined through the centuries.

Where does this royal dignity originate? It is your deepest, authentic self that flows forth when you finally release the cultural programming that so strongly controls your thoughts and actions. Dignity is inherent in all living beings and especially within human beings; the sense of innate worth we have gives rise to unconditional love, compassion, and all of the noblest qualities that are associated with humanity. Religions have many names for this dignity, but it doesn't really matter what we call it. We just need to realise that it exists throughout all of life, and it is our true source of authentic being. To recognize our own dignity is to acknowledge that we are worthy of unconditional love—a love that is not dependent on our physical appearance, intellectual ability, nationality, age, socioeconomic status, or even our behaviours.

That last item may require further explanation. How can we be dignified if we choose to act dishonourably by taking actions such as lying or stealing, or more subtle behaviours such as thinking badly about ourselves or others? Well, let us remember that our dignity is our true essence, never stained by our behaviours. Our actions are controlled by our thinking, and the way we think is quite important, as it creates beliefs about who we are and the world we inhabit. If we truly embraced our innate dignity, then we would have no negative thoughts about ourselves or others, and our harmful actions would diminish. So, individuals who appear to act in ways contrary to their dignity actually believe in a thought program that is dysfunctional—but they don't realise it.

To embrace our natural dignity is to give ourselves permission to see and feel these false beliefs more deeply. Capturing the original feelings that occurred when they were created is critical to releasing their hold on us. This is like returning a gold yoke that formerly limited our capacity for freedom back into the fire. The gold is transformed into a crown of dignity.

Why does feeling the original emotions help to release the blame-game programming? Because each recurring negative thought pattern originates from a particular scene in life in which the original emotion was not released. This emotion is literally stuffed down into our energy fields (see the Introduction for Brennan's explanation) where it then blocks our naturally flowing energy and eventually creates some form of disease in our minds and bodies. If, however, we focus attention on the emotions underlying the thoughts rather than follow the usual pattern of playing out the negative story, we can actually begin to contact the "gold," and that can be reshaped in the fire of our awareness. When we embrace the feeling rather than repress it as we did previously, the energy in ourselves changes.

Often the emotions associated with a traumatic event may unveil themselves only over a period of time, with successive layers revealing slight variations of feeling as we move deeper towards the core. For example, we may first experience rage, then sadness, and then perhaps later more anger, shame, and fear, followed by deep sadness. Through each stage, if we allow such feelings to emerge and choose not to judge ourselves in the process, then the shadow, or unaccepted side of our nature, will be healed.

Just prior to my plunge into depression, a plethora of emotions began emerging; it was like a horde of ants swarming over a fresh kill—so much so that I was overwhelmed and went into a state of high anxiety, physically and mentally. I felt (and literally was) out of control. This was the extreme price I paid for the many years of emotional suppression. I hadn't intentionally chosen to keep such a tight lid on my feelings; it was simply a consequence of my blame-game programming and my early childhood experiences. Because I had believed that being a good person meant not expressing my authentic self, I acted out what I was taught as a child and continued to believe that keeping thoughts and feelings to myself was more acceptable than letting them out.

When you repress emotions that are natural to express, you create a shadow to your personality that feels as if it is guilty or shameful. These feelings of unworthiness can exist because of a background story that you tell yourself about your own behaviours that you have negatively judged. These stories are so subtle that they are hard to catch unless you slow down your thoughts enough to catch them as they whiz by. They are like digital files in your mind, running constantly in the background.

This shadow side may emerge occasionally if you're under the influence of drugs or alcohol or under stress. It was stress that caused my shadow side to emerge, and then its presence continued with less intensity as the years went by. The shadow emotions created during trauma in my childhood washed over me like a tidal wave in the initial months, and then as the wave receded, they became less and less powerful.

During these times of extreme emotional release, I learned to embrace myself with unconditional love. At first I would resist the emotions and even berate myself about how wimpy I was, because "I should k(not) be experiencing more emotions about these events!" It was uncomfortable to experience such a stream of emotions on an ongoing basis, and yet I began to feel a change in my energy and well-being that convinced me that these episodes were opening and healing old wounds.

I came to accept that this shadow side of myself was my dear friend, trying to tell me what I needed to know and do to become whole again. The negative feelings I had about myself were really just thought programs about past events along with the repressed emotions they evoked. My innate dignity was always intact, but I hadn't been able to connect with it. I attribute this to my unwillingness to touch the sensitive and hidden side of my vulnerable nature.

When we embrace our innate dignity, we are learning to embrace our shadow selves along with all the nice aspects of ourselves that we accept and feel positive about. This is not the same as making excuses for behaviours that don't meet our values. Rather, it is looking underneath these behaviours to find out if, or why, we may be acting out a blame-game thought program and doing so with a compassionate intention to understand ourselves better.

It is also quite common to project our shadow emotions onto other people and even onto groups and entire societies. That is, we tend to see ourselves as good and see others as bad so that we can maintain an internal sense of righteousness.

However, this scapegoating only perpetuates and deepens the strength of our shadows, and our stories continue to convince us of the validity of our negative thoughts.

There are, of course, elements of society that we generally believe are not healthy and do require change. I believe the key element in how we perceive social problems is one of discerning judgement. Are we judging individuals, or do we see the deeper causes at work in our society that create unhealthy thought programs, leading to difficult circumstances and outcomes? In other words, we need to distinguish between problems that arise from within society itself and those that arise within ourselves. The key is to understand our programming and realise that it often blinds us to the choices that are actually available to us, causing us to feel limited in our capacity to find and make choices.

For many years, my primary vocation was as an environmental scientist. I specialized in researching the environmental factors that impact population-level changes in species. From direct observations in my field studies, it became clear to me that a multitude of conditions need to exist for a single population to grow and, conversely, for it to perish. A species' ability to adapt to the environment cannot occur if it does not know what choices are available to it in regard to alternative food sources or safe refuges. Success depends on whether the species can first of all discover the different choices and then select those that lead to survival.

Choice is what drives our capacity to thrive, survive, or perish in the modern world. Choice, of course, has two aspects: firstly, we must know that we do have choices available to us, and secondly, we must realise that we can choose with free will. A blame-game program creates a limited set of choices around what we see and believe to be possible.

When viewing problems, whether our own or societal, we can choose to look more deeply for underlying causes. When we do, a multitude of solutions may appear. When we're willing to view problems from a choice mentality, then we may bring to the surface our own shadow feelings, which appear as judgements and stories. They will whisper to us, "We can't do anything about it," "Nothing really changes, so why bother?," "People are just that way so get used to it," and so on.

Here we have our first choice in setting an intention to embrace our innate dignity. We can choose to believe that something else is possible rather than accept only the limited set of choices we formerly believed to be available. When the stories and judgements arise, we can give them a voice, recognize them for what they are, and then move into a new space about what might be emerging as a different scenario.

We can set a strong intention to make a choice rather than think and act out of habit. We can choose to think differently. We can choose to know that there are more possibilities even if we're not aware of them at the time. We can choose to allow our stories to play through without believing in them or acting them out. We can choose to allow everything while staying in our dignity.

Staying in our dignity is about realising our goodness and then choosing to act from that core belief rather than from the blame-game thoughts that come into our heads. Think of it like wearing a velvet-padded royal crown—it might feel a bit awkward at first, but then it gets to feel nice and warm and very special.

When we begin to assume the royal crown of dignity, then we can more easily see the dignity in all beings—first human, then animals, and eventually all living things (even slime molds and lawyers).

Life flows more easily when you're *aligned with* your *divine dignity* that has always existed.

Our responsibility is to first embrace our own dignity and then, when we're able, to serve others by recognising theirs. As the flight attendants on airlines say, "Please put on your own oxygen mask before helping others." This is an important guideline in life—one that is worth paying more attention to.

So, here's where we've travelled in this lesson: to reconnect with our authentic selves requires us to begin seeing ourselves as divine beings. This is not about propping up the ego to create an illusion of grandeur. Instead, it is about connecting with our divinity by simply accepting ourselves and our experiences without judgement. Our fears, our regrets, and our current problems are simply messengers pointing the way towards the authenticity we crave.

Embrace dignity means to recognise your innate value and beauty unconditionally—right now, as you are. By embracing your shadow and not believing in your limited stories, you can begin to open up to a choice mentality and its natural abundance.

Value Yourself, Value Others

Can you imagine traveling to a foreign country where no one speaks your language and you don't speak theirs? Even with the best of intentions, it is likely that you would experience many misunderstandings and embarrassments.

Every day, many people experience similar misunderstandings even when they're speaking the same language! Your boss yells at you for forgetting an important client meeting that you swear wasn't on your calendar. Then later that day your partner feels hurt by your lack of enthusiasm for attending a party hosted by a friend whom you find to be absolutely obnoxious.

We instinctively believe that when words are spoken or written, then total communication instantly happens. Yet, communication is much more than words; in addition to the words we choose, it incorporates our intention, our tone of voice, our body language, and our actions before or after what we say.

Imagine this scene: Your best friend says, "We'll definitely come to your barbecue on Saturday." Then, on the day of the party, he calls to present his apologies and offers some lame excuse. This is the third time it has happened in the last two months, and you're beginning to wonder if he's perhaps got better things to do than spend time with you.

Rather than get upset, you could attempt to understand his behaviour. This can be challenging, as we often find it difficult to understand other people or to be understood by them. After struggling with this issue in my personal and professional life, I have come to see that our capacity to communicate is based upon a use of language that often disempowers people instead of empowering them.

For example, in the above scenario, when your friend tells you at first that he intends to come to your barbecue, is he really meaning it or just pretending? It could be both. What if he really does feel keen to see us but also has a need to spend time with his new girlfriend who lives two hours away, which means he can only visit her on the weekend? If so, his excuse is real and not a snub at all. So, what prevents him from saying this more clearly?

The way we use our English language, alongside our blame-game programming, is often based on fear, guilt, and manipulation rather than love, trust, and empowerment. In the above example, your best friend is afraid to let you know that he has a strong need to spend time with the new woman, as he wants to appear self-determined. However, if he faced his real feelings about the situation—namely, that he wants to see his girlfriend but, at the same time, doesn't want to lose your respect or friendship—then he could be honest and tell you about his real feelings and needs. In other words, he could remove the mask of trying to please you.

In this scenario, if both individuals were clear about their own feelings and could communicate to each other about what they valued, then it would be a straightforward matter to have a conversation and thereby develop a creative strategy for alternate ways of sharing time together (perhaps getting together in the evening for a beer or working out together at the gym).

One of the most important discoveries I've made in recent years (besides learning to like Vegemite) is that our language conditions how we see ourselves and the world. If we truly want to live in the flow of a more authentic life, then a critical step is to use a more life-affirming language.

As with most things, there is not one single correct path. I can only share what has worked for me and suggest that you test whatever seems to attract you. As I was beginning to value myself more, I started to learn a new way of relating to others that is counter to what most of us were taught. I read many books on communication, but the approach that had a strong impact upon me and led me to take a course from its author, Marshall Rosenberg, was called *Nonviolent Communication*. This truly revolutionary approach allows us to dismantle our negative mental programming and replace it with a "language of life" in which we take full responsibility for our own selves.

The key foundation for living in a world of authenticity and abundance is to understand that we are completely responsible for our lives. We can only respond to another person via our own free will—whether it is through our thoughts, our emotions, our actions, or any combination of these.

Valuing ourselves is not the same as being selfish. The difference can be seen if we ask the question, "Do we only see ourselves when we think of life issues, or do we also consider the perspective of others?" I believe that valuing ourselves *and* valuing others is what makes for a real relationship. If we ask, "How can both of us meet our needs?" rather than simply "How can I meet mine?" then we're seeing solutions in a world of abundance. In using the word *needs* I am referring to the basic physical, emotional, mental, and spiritual values that support us in our lives.

Another important point is that we may decide, in certain situations, to put another person's needs ahead of ours or even to put our own needs first. If we make either choice consciously, and after attempting to find solutions to meet the needs of all concerned, then that decision is a life-affirming choice.

Learning to value ourselves is to first communicate lovingly with ourselves. Are we listening to and understanding our emotions or do we jump straight away to blaming ourselves for our situation? If we create love within ourselves first, then we are more likely to be capable of expressing clearly to another our feelings and needs, and of hearing, in a nonjudgemental way, the meaning behind their words.

A Tibetan lama whom I once met remarked that Westerners were "using busyness as a form of laziness." This statement struck me as odd at first and then later, after I'd given it a great deal of thought, as very wise. Why do we often stay so busy? I recently took some time out in my life, and I can say that idleness isn't as glamorous as we often think. Sitting around contemplating oneself and one's situation brings up all kinds of muck from the bottom of the pond!

What I discovered in that time of non-work was that until that time, I had used busyness as a form of not truly valuing myself. When I was distracted with all kinds of interesting (and sometimes boring) projects, relationship dramas, and money issues, I never really had to spend any time with myself. I didn't value the time of stillness and silence, because I was actually scared of what I might feel if I did stop doing anything for too long.

The laziness is the avoidance of taking time to actually see and feel what is happening in ourselves and in our lives. I didn't value myself enough to want to take that time to understand and hear what my authentic voice might say. It probably would have said, "Will you stop all this nonsense and start paying attention to my real needs?"

Now, I'm grateful for the space that became available in my life when I was not distracted by the normal nine-to-five work week. During this time I learned to value myself and to hear what my entire being had to say. I've learned that our bodies and our feelings are excellent indicators of our general state, and if we pay attention to those aspects of ourselves, then we can prevent larger problems from escalating. *How well do you listen to your emotional, spiritual, and physical needs?*

Learning to value ourselves, which leads to truly valuing others, is to begin communicating in a life-affirming and non-judgemental way so that we can become responsible for our own well-being. Reconnecting with what is truly important to us is the first step in creating circumstances and choosing relationships that honour that uniqueness.

Value yourself, value others means investigating new ways of communicating that honour you and the other person at the same time.

Strategies Are K(not) Needs

As children, we begin learning strategies to get our needs met right away. For example: a baby knows that if she cried, her mother will come to see what's wrong. In this case, the strategy is to cry, and the need may be anything from being hungry to feeling afraid. The baby uses the same strategy to meet her various needs, as it's the only one she knows and initially appears to work quite well. Then, as more learning takes place, the little baby starts assimilating cues for what is allowable as a strategy and what is not. Behavioural reinforcement occurs, and the child begins to form mental, emotional, and physical habits.

One key mental habit that became very strong for me as a child was the gratifying habit of pleasing others. It was reinforced early that if I did good things for others, then they would do good things for me (and would prevent bad things from happening). Of course, this seems to be a simple type of behaviour reinforcement, and one that is pretty benign. However, when behaviours that perhaps should not be reinforced actually are, then these behaviours become engrained in our psyche. Later in life, such behaviours can become problematic.

When I was a young girl, I wanted desperately to please my mother, as she seemed to already have a burden of problems. She was a single mum and not handling life all that well. I would try not to bother her with my own problems, as she was consumed with dealing with her own personal and financial issues. My need at the time was to maintain peace and try to keep the love flowing between us.

As I grew into an adult, this strategy of keeping everything to myself was used with other people, which wasn't so bad for them initially but ended up being somewhat disastrous for me and unhealthy for my relationships. I thought I could only be loved by being silent about my own problems; therefore, I didn't really know how to share my needs—let alone know what they might be! I had confused a *strategy* of keeping peace with a *need*—yet my real needs for connection were not being met in my relationships, and it took me many years to come to understand why. I had lost my ability to connect and express from my authentic self in order to have acceptance from others (and feel accepting of myself).

Before we continue to explore this topic, let's explain the difference between a need (or value) versus a strategy. *A need* is something we value and that is important to us either in the moment or in the long term. These needs have been categorised by a well-known psychologist into what is known as 'Maslow's hierarchy of needs', which begins with basic-level needs and then continues on to the more refined needs, such as self-actualisation (or what I call an authentic life). Our basic needs are generally physical: food, water, safety, and shelter. Our more complex needs involve other people and include belonging, love, and connection, as well as the ability to create and express one's true self. What is interesting about these universal needs is that they are common to persons everywhere in the world. This seems to be the case regardless of socioeconomic and cultural background.

A strategy is a way to get our needs met. For example, perhaps we enjoy unwinding at the end of the day through laughter and fun. This need for enjoyment could be met by using many different strategies, including spending time with family or friends, entertaining oneself (kids are great at this), reading a light-hearted book, or watching a funny comedy show or movie.

One of the most important lessons I've learned is not to mix up needs with strategies. We can get into serious trouble if we do so. In fact, all conflict is really about different needs, but often, the two or more parties become focused instead on strategies, and that creates defensiveness and tension. I believe that all conflict could be resolved if only people were to focus on the needs of each party with an open heart and mind.

Getting to know our needs is the key, and it does take some practice, as I've learned. I used to confuse all kinds of strategies with needs. At one time, I believed that I needed sex, needed approval, needed to be thought of as a nice person, and so forth. Yet, when I looked into these supposed needs more closely, what I discovered was that underneath each one, there were more complex needs. Take, for example, sex. Yes, of course, the physical act can bring profound pleasure. But what I discovered was that I actually wanted intimacy—the feeling of knowing and being known by another person deeply. Intimacy may or may not be a component of sex. It is most readily found through learning to openly communicate with oneself and with others.

In modern society, it is easy to confuse needs with strategies. In fact, many marketing folks attempt to do just that in their advertising campaigns. The main focus in advertising is to create a sense that this item will fulfill your need to be something more than you already are or to feel better about yourself. Yet, ultimately, how we feel about ourselves cannot depend on the outer material aspects of life, no matter how delicious these bits are to us. Even if we enjoy beautiful clothes, well-made tools, or racy cars, we can still realise that these items are strategies and not needs.

Let's go back to our earlier example of wanting to enjoy some fun after work. Most people in the Western world own a television and watch it for several hours each night. I'm a rare person who believes that television is not a useful strategy for meeting my personal needs for learning and entertainment. My needs for relaxation, education, and fun are met so well in other ways. Without a television, I spend more time with my partner and friends, and I enjoy reading interesting books, writing, or occasionally watching a movie. By the way, I have one friend who also doesn't own a television, so there must be a movement starting!

Seriously, though, I suggest we try out new strategies for getting our needs met instead of just relying on the same old ones. It can add a bit of spice to our lives as well.

Strategies are k(not) needs means stop being on autopilot and start knowing what's really important to you. Then you can create a diversity of strategies to fulfil everyone's needs.

Be Real, Act with Zeal

Life sometimes presents us with a good wallop on the head, maybe from a low-lying branch or a mistaken identity with our thoughts. I got a strong lesson about my life when my misleading perceptions about myself crashed into the reality of my authentic self. In current terminology, the name given to this experience is clinical depression, and apparently a significant number of adults and children experience it at least once in their lifetime. Depression is a frightening, debilitating, and quite misunderstood disease of this modern age.

Why do I say that my depression was caused by a direct confrontation between my misperceptions and my reality? Earlier in the book, we discussed the proposition that blame-game programming is the basis for creating a higher potential for depression in our Western culture. My theory is that depression is more likely to occur when our blame-game programming becomes incessant in our brain, creating beliefs and feelings that we're extremely limited in our options to change this extremely limited world. As I've already stated, please don't place too much stock in my opinion, because I'm not a medical doctor or psychologist. However, if it rings true for you, then perhaps you might explore these ideas for yourself.

Here's a description of the crash scene prior to the depression. I was working like a dog at a job that didn't align with my values, and my boss was downright hostile. Yet, I still believed that I could and should not complain or take stronger actions to help myself. I ignored my body screaming for rest (thinking I should not take time out for myself) and my spirit melting from a lack of support (thinking I did not need help). Instead, I kept going until the karma (reality) train ran over my dogma (false beliefs about myself and the world).

What was the big lesson for me from this event?

It was: *be real, act with zeal.*

Why are we not authentic in relating to ourselves and to other people, and how can we be more so? Firstly, we want to be loved so much that we sometimes pretend or lie (especially to ourselves) about what we truly value. This occurs when our shadows (made up of our feelings of shame, guilt, or sadness) are not allowed to come forth, and we create a false sense of self. We can create masks of our true thoughts and feelings if we are afraid to express ideas about ourselves. For example, if I unconsciously believe that I'm unworthy because my father repeatedly yelled at me as a child, then I wear a mask of unworthiness. I then unconsciously grasp for other's love and approval, and in doing so I surrender my needs to those of others to get that love.

In my case, the unconscious beliefs that led to my depression were the following:

1. I should k(not) focus too much on myself. This meant:
   o Others' needs came before my own.
   o My value was based on the perceptions of others rather than my own.
   o I didn't value the wisdom or health of my body.
2. I should k(not) ask other people for help with my problems.

You can clearly see how both of these beliefs are interrelated, as they are both in the category of: "I should not bother people, as I don't value myself too highly." Creating masks to cover our real selves is a gradual process that occurs through life; therefore, it may take some time to remove the masks. In time, they become part of our identity that we hold quite dear. When we devalue ourselves, we often feel that we're imposing on other people by asking for our needs to be met, even if they are perfectly willing to help!

Remember that needs are key aspects of our lives that we value. For example, we may hold integrity as a key need in our lives, and each day we try to live it by being clear about our intentions and acting and speaking in alignment with them. One of the key thought programs of a blame-game culture is that because we're not enough in ourselves, then we are constantly looking to other people to satisfy our needs, although we often don't want to directly ask them. Instead, we often try bargaining for our needs, which is extremely common in society. "If you give me need X (what I need), then I'll give you need Y (what you need)." Does this sound familiar?

When we give or receive from a bargaining interchange, we're in a precarious position because we can feel disturbed if the other person doesn't deliver what we ordered. We then become disappointed, angry, and perhaps even resentful that what was promised isn't being given. The tricky part comes when we realise that we might not ever get what we want in the way we want it—at least not from other people.

This is when really big bargaining comes in. Are we going to bargain with ourselves and compromise our values to stick with a certain situation or stay with a particular person because doing so meets some, but not all, of our values? If we do continue in the same circumstance, then we may begin to mask our true needs and true selves, and this can initiate a pattern that eventually compromises not only our authentic selves, but also our spiritual, mental, and physical well-being.

Of course, we say, everyone must compromise in some way. Perhaps. But we must take into account the degree to which we're willing to push down our deepest values and for how long. Sometimes we might do it for a certain reason and for a limited length of time. But then what if we do it again and again? What are the consequences, and how do we then begin to feel about ourselves?

If we're not very conscious of our needs, then it is quite easy to bargain, because it doesn't seem like a trade-off. However, we might still have resentful thoughts later. We can act as though we're being good people in meeting others' needs at the expense of our own. Yet, inside we know that it's a poor bargain, and we squirm each time we don't acknowledge our own values more clearly.

Therefore, becoming aware of our deepest values is the first step in being real. If honesty is important to us, as it should be, then we're going to have to take off the mask and be brutally honest with ourselves about what we really believe. Are we really all that keen about our jobs, our current partners, or our current lifestyles? Why do we enjoy them or why do we not? What values are being lived and which are only partially or not at all?

When, finally, we have a sense of what is truly meaningful in our lives, we can align our words and actions with our real cores. No more bargaining, even for the smallest stuff. If our masks are removed (often gradually), then yes, we might disappoint, anger, and even lose people who are currently in our lives. But then again, we might just gain friends who are more aligned with our values and who like us just the way we are! More importantly, we will also respect ourselves more, because we had to take courageous steps to: 1) first know what is important to us, and 2) act on that knowledge. This is being truly at home with ourselves and with the world. So what if we might appear a bit strange to others? It's not the end of the world—in fact, it might just be the beginning of a new and more authentic world.

When we're real, our entire beings vibrate with greater potency, and events tend to conspire to help us rather than hinder us. Does being real mean doing exactly what we feel like? This is another sticky point. No, it doesn't. We remember the lesson about human dignity. This means respecting ourselves *and* respecting others. Just because we really like walking around nude in public doesn't mean we have the right to do so! However, we might look for a nudist colony where we can feel comfortable and express our true selves.

When we're comfortable with ourselves and know what floats our boats, then we can act from our core values and make clearer, more deliberate choices.

To act with *zeal* is to move confidently towards our life values and to say no when situations arise that conflict with those values. And then to say yes to the opportunities that align with our core selves.

Here are some of my personal key life values: authenticity, honesty, beauty, connection, creativity, and joy. When I'm affirming these values through my thoughts and actions, then I feel most fulfilled. What are yours?

Be real, act with zeal means that everyone is unique, and only through taking off your mask and knowing who you really are can you serve your greatest purpose and fulfil your deepest values.

Carry Tissues and a Wrench

I am a well-trained Campfire Girl (similar to Girl Scouts), and so I try to be prepared for potential catastrophes like a dress popping a button just before I am about to walk into the church as a bridesmaid at my best friend's wedding. (Yes, this did happen to me.) When we gained beads in

Campfire Girls—which indicated skills or behaviours that we'd demonstrated—they would be sewn onto our vests in an artistic pattern, and thus we would proudly wear our badges of honour on our chests. These beads might represent friendship, woodworking, helpfulness, and the like, displaying the kinds of activities and qualities we'd demonstrated for all to see.

As a woman growing up in an American family, I learned through my cultural programming that I was in this world to serve others. I don't think that boys are inculcated with this cultural norm quite so strongly. They may even be given the opposite impression—that they should help themselves first (develop skills to compete against their mates).

Recently, it has come to my attention that to become a more balanced person, someone who integrates both feminine and masculine aspects and actions, it is necessary to take stock of what one believes. You must ask yourself if your values are really your own. If they are not, then it is important to see how you might include additional perspectives that could enhance your sense of authenticity.

If I were a parent of a Campfire Girl and currently engaged in the training and handing out of beads for today's youth, then I'd add a few more beads to the collection, including serve ourselves and serve others.

As we explored in prior sections, it is sometimes easy for us to fall into one of the two camps of *either* serving ourselves *or* serving others. Remember how girls are taught to be thoughtful and kind and not selfish, and boys are told to compete and be successful.

Actually, both serving others and serving ourselves can compromise our deepest values *if taken to extremes*. We might think about what we've been willing to do within the past year and ask ourselves if we feel any shame or even some slight discomfort about it. Bargaining away our values can occur whenever we don't come from a place of honesty when serving, whether it is ourselves or another.

We bargain when we want to avoid our shadows—those difficult aspects of our inner emotions and thought patterns that we fear the most. If we've had trauma associated with the expression of our feelings, then the female aspect of self will be suppressed; alternately, when we haven't been able to assert our independence, then the male side will be less vibrant.

An integration of male and female aspects can occur in individuals without changing the physical or sexual identity of a person. I personally believe this is how we become more whole. Doing so enables us to stop projecting our shadow sides onto others, especially those of the opposite sex.

I recently took a quiz that was in a book about the differences in communication styles among men and women. The quiz was a tool to determine how a person's overall brain pattern is wired—highly male, highly female, or somewhere in between. I came out almost exactly in the middle, which wasn't that surprising to me. If I'd taken the same quiz about fifteen years ago, I could say with some confidence that it would have indicated a more male brain, as that was my personality at the time.

In my younger adulthood, I didn't relate highly to feminine qualities and images. The male world was far more interesting to me than the frilly, gossipy, non-intellectual living style that I saw in many women. Of course, here I am being deliberately judgemental, as that is how my mind would have summarised my thoughts at the time. In truth, I was fearful of the feminine. From childhood experiences, femininity had brought me only grief and difficulty, and I consciously moved away from experiencing those aspects of life. Because of my past experiences, I harboured a deep shadow that was almost too painful to acknowledge. Thus, it lay dormant until my early thirties.

I even chose a generally male-dominated career in science and discarded my potential as an artist and writer because I viewed those particular pursuits as too impractical. I became extremely obsessed about knowledge and rational thought, because I believed they offered me a more secure basis for understanding the world (and myself). Although I had always been keen on exploring the nature of mind, I did so initially from a rational, scientific perspective. I will admit, however, that my explorations into the mind also included Eastern metaphysical philosophy.

The transition towards my feminine-feeling heart started in my mid-thirties, and it is now almost fully integrated into my male-thinking head. Feeling from the heart is not traditionally taught at school or university, and yet it is an integral way of being that allows us to relate to ourselves with compassion. I can say that some women I've met don't have this feminine heart very much, and some men have it quite strongly, so it is not about the physical form. It is more dependent on our early cultural and family experiences, as well as how conscious and authentic we have become.

We can't change our past, but thankfully, we can change the programming from our past! Scientists are confirming the plasticity of our brains in terms of the capacity to rewire our mental models and even our physiological states, and this is good news. Yes, changing our programming does take patience and effort. But then, what worthwhile endeavor doesn't?

As of now, we can choose to integrate ourselves as whole beings, and I'd like to illustrate the male and female aspects of our beings through the metaphors of a *wrench* (or *spanner* if you're in Britain or Australia) and *tissues*.

The wrench is a symbol for the rational view of life for which the brain can be our symbol. It represents the constant barrage of physical change that occurs to us and around us on a daily basis. The dog has eaten our treasured diamond earring, or we just got a flat tire on the way to a job interview! Are we capable of approaching these disruptions in our lives with awareness and practical how-to, regardless of whether they are caused by our own recklessness?

Rationality is a wonderful tool that enables us to disassemble complex situations, as well as the physical world, into their respective components while maintaining an understanding of each part's relative importance. The human capacity for understanding and modifying our environments to suit our particular needs is unparalleled in the animal kingdom.

When our brains are trained to think rationally, we are able to develop both practical and theoretical approaches for clarifying issues and acting in the material world. Problem solving is regarded as a male trait primarily because men generally enjoy the mental gyrations of analytically picking apart a complex issue. Of course, many women enjoy this activity as well, and so what I'm referring to is really the nature of the individual's brain, not the physical appearance.

A wrench is therefore necessary, because every person faces the need to use practical, rationally based problem solving on a daily basis. It has probably become our society's tool of choice, as it brings enhanced physical comfort and a sense of control into our human lives.

Along with a sturdy wrench, it is critical to have, ever ready, a packet of tissues. I used to think that duct tape was the second best item, but now I've discovered that tissues are far more useful for all types of unexpected events.

Tissues represent our ability to give and receive empathy, and that quality is symbolized by the heart. Empathy takes a more compassionate view than sympathy, which at times verges on pity. Empathy can only be achieved when a person is understood and accepted fully for what he's feeling and not judged in any way. It is, to put it another way, like stepping into another person's shoes. Importantly, this principle of empathy applies foremost to ourselves with the aim of not becoming attached or stuck in an emotion.

Are we able to give ourselves and others empathy when required? As Campfire Girls, we were trained to give first aid, and I would now recommend that we train all girls and boys in giving first-aid empathy—first to oneself (remember the empathic welcome mat) and then to others.

For example, your girlfriend of ten years has just dumped you for a younger, better-looking guy. You initially blame yourself. You believe the cause was your extra weight (was another twenty kilograms too much?) and the long weeks you spent working away from home because your boss's approval was more important than your own. You may feel that you're unworthy to have another relationship because of your deep regrets about losing your girlfriend.

Now where is the self-empathy in that? Yes, of course you probably did make mistakes. However, empathy is not about ignoring the mistakes but fully embracing the needs behind them. You did have a strong need to keep up good relations with the boss, and yes, your eating habits weren't great, but you did at least *try* to spend more time with her than at the gym. So, perhaps there were some pretty good reasons behind what you did at the time. However, the fact that you're now alone isn't so wonderful, and perhaps you could give yourself some empathy (heart hugs) in relation to your sadness and grief.

Once you've given yourself lots of tissues, then the time will come when you'll want to take a better look at your behaviours and needs and ask how you might more authentically meet what appear to be conflicting needs. Maybe you can't get your girlfriend back, but you can act more responsibly in the future for the next girlfriend. This might include developing the confidence to say no to the boss and then developing an improved life-work balance.

Because we are biological beings in a society that requires us to have sexual identities, we may often overemphasize the mindset of being male or female. Of course, we are biological entities, and this directly influences how we see ourselves. Yet, as we move closer to the truth of who we really are, we can loosen our attachment to our socially defined roles and focus on being whole and authentic beings. We can begin to allow ourselves to skillfully use both a wrench and a tissue!

Carry tissue and wrench means integrating your masculine and feminine aspects. To be a good friend to yourself and to others, you can practice the skills of empathy and rational thinking.

Practices for Chapter 3

Reconnect: Claim Your Authentic Being

Practice 1

1. Let yourself feel whatever is occurring in your body and mind without making any judgement about it. Practice now and notice if you are still judging any feeling or thought. Judgements are useful, so don't judge the judgement! Embrace everything equally while allowing

for new possibilities to arise, whether they are thoughts, feelings, or actions.

2. Three times a day, stop and notice your own dignity for three minutes. Feel your innate worthiness by focusing on a recent action that you feel happy about in your life.

Practice 2

1. Next time you become annoyed with someone, try asking, "What is it that I would prefer to happen and why?" Let yourself feel the why part for a while and then pretend that you can do something to create the preferred outcome. How do you feel now, knowing you can do something about it? Now see if you can take a small step towards that outcome.

2. When you are feeling quite good about yourself, take a few minutes to simply be aware of what's happening within you. What has made you feel so good? Take the time to reflect on what has created this feeling and make a mental commitment to create more of this experience for yourself.

Practice 3

1. Write down your core life values and notice if they are values or strategies. If they are strategies (like wealth creation), then see if you can determine the underlying values.

2. Next to each value, write how you're currently living this value, or if you're not, then write how you would like to live that value now. Try to keep it simple so that you can take an action immediately.

Practice 4

To integrate more fully your masculine and feminine aspects, try one or both of the following exercises:

1. When someone starts crying, do you feel awkward and try to get them to stop, or do you allow them to spill it all out? If the former, then perhaps let them speak for a while without interrupting and notice what feelings come up for you.

2. Next time life throws you a problem, notice how you react to it. Do you believe you can handle it yourself (without anyone's help), do you ask for help if it's beyond your capabilities, or do you jump to get help without trying solutions yourself? If you don't usually ask for help, try asking for it. If you generally do ask, then try doing it all yourself and notice how it feels.

CHAPTER 4

Key 3 – Release

Let Go to Let Your Authentic Life Flow

Although I currently live on the big southern island called Australia, I am an American citizen born and bred. I still feel a lot of love for my home country, especially in these difficult times when so many people are suffering hardships. As people deal with ongoing change, they may easily slip into blame-game judgements even more than they usually would. This is a sign that there is a lot of pain, as we criticise others or ourselves in order to ease our pain, at least temporarily.

Growing up in the United States in a lower-middle-class family, I formed the belief that I didn't need support from other people and that I could overcome the difficulties of living with sheer hard work. I was a really devoted worker, working full time from the age of sixteen and attending college at night for many years to eventually obtain my bachelor's degree. I felt proud of how hard I had worked to try to realise the American dream. My thoughts were that I had to prove my worth and that I couldn't expect the world to simply meet my needs without hard work. I couldn't just enjoy life and somehow be rewarded for doing nothing more.

Did that belief help or hinder me? I suppose it made me ambitious, which has both a positive and a negative side. I felt that my efforts were focused on actions that would be worthwhile for me and also for the world at large. Yet, I was subconsciously accepting the blame-game programming that told me I wasn't powerful enough to create my life in a way that balanced work and enjoyment. I didn't take a vacation for more than two weeks in any year until I moved to Australia at the age of thirty-seven. That's probably the case for many other Americans who are plagued by a strong work ethic (and workplaces that only give two weeks' vacation) to such a degree that it limits their enjoyment of life.

I still struggle with feelings of "too much" enjoyment and even "too much" free time! I have often wondered why some people work such long hours when they don't actually need the money. I know that for many people working long hours is about getting the bills paid. I'm talking about the high proportion of the middle- to upper-income group who work extra hours when they could almost certainly get by with less money. Are they driven by the same mental blame-game program that I was? Do they actually enjoy working so much? I'm quite curious to know, so if you are among that group, please write and tell me your stories and beliefs. (See About the Author for contact details.)

I'm not judging the amount of time people devote to work as good or bad but simply questioning their motives for putting in lengthy amounts of time for their work. I quite enjoy the career I'm now in as a small business owner, and my intention is to keep it that way and to ensure that my motivation for doing my work is one of love and not fear.

Uncovering our basic motivation is an important focus in becoming more authentic. Often, we are driven by our fears rather than by a strong sense of trust and engagement with a world that is supportive and loving.

Perhaps our minds have subconsciously formed beliefs that having basic food, shelter, safety, health, good relationships, and satisfying livelihoods are not enough. We must also have entertainment, good clothes, nice cars, a fancy house, and so forth—even though these items don't actually contribute all that much to our basic well-being. Again, I'm not judging these items as bad, as I'm known to like the comforts of nice things myself. What I'm pointing out is the confusion we create for ourselves when we mix up our sense of self-worth with the idea of either an abundance of physical goods or a lack thereof.

Our outer circumstances do not reflect who we truly are. If we begin to realise this truth, then the changes in our material world become less significant to our feelings of innate self-worth. If, on the other hand, we cannot separate ourselves from our worldly goods, then we create our own illusion that the world is, or is not, giving us what we need. When we have the mindset that the world is not giving us what we need, then we develop a sense of scarcity, and fear becomes a dominant feature of our thinking.

What if a person believed that the world was supportive and that he had, in his possession, all the resources necessary for him to create the destiny he desired? Would that assist him in developing strength and courage to face any type of adversity? It sure wouldn't hurt. Of course, it is also critical to face the facts and be honest about a situation. However, that doesn't in any way exclude the mindset that we can overcome adverse circumstances and temporary setbacks.

The next set of lessons for facing and overcoming this particular k(not) of not trusting the world will focus on some pretty big issues. I suggest you come back to these again and again, as they are not as simple as they might first appear. Test them out for yourself and also try writing about your experiences in a journal so you're the one deciding what's really true.

Trust

I'd like you to trust me when I say that this lesson is the most important, so pay attention. Of course, you won't really trust me, will you? We've only just met, and it often takes quite a lot of time and experience to create trust. I know that's true for most people, although I'd like to speed it up for us, so I'll explain why trust is such an important life lesson in terms of living an authentic life.

Trust is essential to the truth, just as the sun is the source of light. Most of the time, we don't really trust ourselves, let alone other people or the world in general. I mean real trust, not just 99.9 percent trust, but complete, no-fingers-crossed, no-holding-back trust. What, then, is that kind of trust?

I really can't answer that fully, but I'd say that asking the question is actually far more important than finding the answer. What does complete trust mean? Does it mean acceptance? Does it mean surrender? Perhaps it demands an understanding that everything we do ourselves can be trusted implicitly, and everything everyone else does can be trusted too. Even when we experience pain, we can trust the pain to be guiding us, and we can trust ourselves to listen to our inner wisdom so we may act from our authentic being.

How can we trust what we usually label as bad? We can choose to ask this question of ourselves and see what answers emerge. I won't answer it here, because any words I write might be taken too literally or might not fully apply to other sets of circumstances than my own. I'd like to suggest that we see this questioning as a personal experiment. We should trust ourselves to be willing to ask the big questions and then trust that answers will come.

What would happen if we trusted everything in life? This doesn't mean that we let people treat us badly or that anything we do is simply okay. Trust emerges when we let go of our moralising judgements and simply act from a source of authenticity. If someone is yelling at you, instead of judging that person as a loud-mouthed idiot, you could try accepting him as he is and then trusting that: 1) you can speak your truth respectfully and without judgement, and 2) whatever happens after that can be trusted.

What feelings arise when I suggest that you trust everything? Do you fear a loss of control? Or perhaps you don't see the point of this exercise, and you feel sort of inert about the whole question. You might experience a feeling of non-committal or depression (a lack of any feeling at all). These are all still feelings, and every feeling has a reason for being present, as it can help us to uncover the story that limits who we think we are.

The main point is to know if the question evokes some feeling of curiosity in you and/or if there's a feeling of fear holding you back. Just be as clear as possible about both of these feelings. Can you trust yourself enough to move into the question while also accepting the reasons for holding back? It seems like a dilemma, but it's actually related to having dual needs (and dueling with them). It may seem impossible to meet them simultaneously, but it's important to recognise them all the same.

This is the reason why we often have difficulty trusting: on the one hand we say yes to an aspect of the situation, but on the other hand we are not completely comfortable with it, so there is a conflict inside that limits our sense of trust.

Even to trust the nature of this dilemma is a great beginning. You may ask, "What if I make a mistake?" Well, what is a mistake but a lesson in disguise? I'll try explaining why mistakes can be virtuous and important to our reprogramming.

We often live from a very unconscious set of beliefs, and as we have noted throughout this book, these thought programs limit who and what we believe ourselves (and the world) to be. The results of these beliefs will manifest themselves in our lives as experiences and feelings, some that we like and also some that we dislike. The ones we feel negativity towards point to those areas in our programming that are unconscious, and these are really disguised lessons waiting to be learned.

Trusting that our feelings have a useful role is one key insight. Emotional pain is simply pointing us to unconscious and unhealthy belief systems about our lives. The role of emotions is to assist us with bringing these blame-game thoughts into our consciousness where they can be healed through release of the deeper feelings. Trust is a way of speeding up the process. Like a high-speed broadband connection, it connects us to a direct understanding of this present moment—which is the only place that healing can begin.

Trust and what, in religion, is called faith may be similar concepts, although I'd like to differentiate the two because blind faith can cause us to relinquish access to our authentic selves. Importantly, when we begin to recognise our authentic nature, a direct understanding arises that is not based on intellectual reasoning or limited stories. Eventually, it also becomes easier to relinquish our judgemental thoughts that previously would take over and create a sense of fear and loss of control. Therefore, trust is sensing our inner knowing for ourselves by spending time listening to our quiet and authentic selves.

Often, we seek out advice from people who probably don't understand us or, if they do, might have their own agendas that interfere with truly helping us. I'm talking about inner self-reliance as a form of trust. This doesn't limit our capacity to ask for others' opinions or views; it simply maintains the final determinant of our decision making within ourselves.

Self-reliance is not the same as independence (though they are related), but rather a clarity of mind and of heart that relies upon its own guidance. Physical self-reliance is its least important aspect, although it may be useful for our growth and development. Mental and spiritual self-reliance are vital to our experiencing trust and, therefore, becoming trustworthy ourselves.

Mental self-reliance is being willing to open up to the unconscious shadows within and to become friends with each one (therefore learning the lesson it has to teach us). Owning our emotions and becoming responsible for our actions are two ways in which we begin to establish ourselves as reliable and authentic persons. In becoming self-reliant, we also become more responsible in our words and in our actions. People begin to trust us more, even though our perspectives may differ from theirs. Honest discussion is a hallmark of great trust and is a valuable result of two authentic people sharing their inner worlds.

Trust is becoming mentally and spiritually self-reliant. It's being willing to accept everything as it is, while being true to yourself.

Life Is But a Dream!

Have you ever been dreaming and simultaneously realised that you're in a dream? If you can catch yourself in the dream, then it is easy to leap five-metre fences, a feat that would seem impossible in our normal waking state. More commonly, we only recognise the dream as a visual illusion when we awaken from our sleeping state.

In the normal awake state, we have sensory information coming into our field of perception. The senses register the data, and the brain begins to interpret its meaning. First, we ask, "What is it (label)?" Then, "What does it mean (evaluation)?" We rely upon our brains' consciousness to continually update us on our changing external and internal realities.

How is the dreaming state any different to our normal awakened state? In our minds, there is no difference, because in a dream we believe the images we sense to be real, even to the point of feeling affected by the images we see, hear, touch, and taste. Yet, after we awaken, we realise that whatever we experienced was not real.

My concept of reality was dramatically shaken by a Tibetan doctor of medicine, who asked a group gathered at one of his workshops, "What if our reality was actually a dream?" This question really stunned me and made me think more deeply about the nature of what we call reality and how we create entire stories around our limited perceptions of the world.

The point that I'm making is that the way we attribute meaning to things, events, and people is based on our mental concepts, not from the objects themselves. For example, two people can often walk away from a conversation and feel quite differently. One could be completely satisfied and the other grumbling about the lack of understanding shown by her friend. Or if you've ever witnessed a crime and then been asked to describe a person involved in it, your perception of his features may not be as accurate as you'd like to believe. Although we rely upon our senses to bring us information about the outer world, the mental concepts we add to this data are only that—concepts.

The life-is-but-a-dream lesson sums up all of the lessons life has to offer by insisting that we lighten up in our attitude towards ourselves, other people, and the continuously moving feast of events. How do we know that we have the "correct" view? We don't. There are as many views in the world as there are people. Of course, we can define our own values and then be willing to maintain our dignity through living those values authentically, but with great respect for others' values as well. Respect for others' viewpoints means that we maintain an attitude that acknowledges their innate dignity, even as we may strongly disagree with the values they espouse.

How might living as though life were a dream change what we do? For me, it means trying new things, whether it be engaging in different thoughts (by asking, "What if I happen to be wrong?"), different approaches (by asking, "What else is possible in this circumstance?"), and different behaviours (by asking, "What could I do that still honours my dignity?").

Think of each day like an experiment—what can you try, change, know, or be that brings greater love, care, understanding, or compassion into your life? Try testing the boundaries of what you believe is right or real. When I say this, I also mean, of course, doing so with great respect to other people.

The line "life is but a dream" comes from that cheery song "Row, Row, Row Your Boat." The verse runs, "Row, row, row your boat / Gently down the stream, / Merrily, merrily, merrily, merrily / Life is but a dream."

My interpretation of this verse is that "your boat" is yourself, and you can "gently" move yourself through life, enjoying the slow, lazy moments and the fast, intense times with equal fervor. After all, this precious moment is all you truly have—the past is a memory, and the future a mirage. In fact, even the present moment quickly disappears and then is no more!

Why do we find it difficult to let go of our expectations and our worries in this present moment? Because they seem to be so real—even if they have never happened! Next time you find yourself worrying about something, try saying out loud, "Life is but a dream." Let whatever is bothering you feel a bit slippery and soft and then ask, "What else is possible?" Just wait, and you'll get an answer.

Another valuable way to let life be less limited and more abundant is to ask, "Who is the dreamer?" This takes us back to the original question at the beginning of this book: who are you? Who is always present and unstained by the swiftly moving currents of emotions and physical sensations? Often, the idea we have of ourselves is quite constrained. "I'm such a perfectionist," "I'm a lazy butt," "I never seem to . . ." and so on. Maybe these characterisations are occasionally correct, but these are still concepts about us that can create an impression that we are unable to be anything else. Can we not let ourselves be playful about who we think we are for a change?

Wake up in the morning and ask, "Who will I be today?" If you're feeling keen to try something new, then state openly what it is you're going to be or do. Perhaps you'd like to reinforce an aspect of yourself that needs encouragement. State it aloud: "I'm an amazingly successful author touching the lives of millions of people!" Hey, that feels great!

Throughout the day, we can also give ourselves reminders whenever events occur that we are tempted to label bad.

Again, if we find ourselves strongly reacting, then we should try noticing the emotions rather than suppressing them. This is where having some distance from our feelings is useful, although not in a detached, cold way but rather from a warm and accepting feeling of care.

When we're connected to the flow of our authentic selves, then it is possible to let go of all of our continual assessments that chatter away in the mind. "He's not good enough," "She's such a weak person," "I'm always so judgemental," blah, blah, blah. We've been conditioned to believe that these thoughts are the truth rather than seeing them for what they are and seeing the story as just a story.

Reminding ourselves that we're in a dream keeps us lighter about our thoughts. Even if strong emotions arise, in our dream state we can give them time and space in a kind way rather than acting them out immediately. This serves to loosen the story before it begins to unravel and trap our minds.

Life is but a dream reminds you to be lighter about thoughts and to give your emotions some breathing room. Be willing to let go of stale and worn stories that no longer serve you.

Be Naked, Be Forgiving

When I was sixteen, I wrote the poem that is at the front of this book. Looking back, I realise that the words contain far more wisdom than I could have known at the time.

Being naked on a glacier is certainly an image of exposure, yet the words of the poem indicate a sense of freedom. It is a paradoxical vision of being completely free and fully open to whatever situation might unfold. I have yearned for that freedom all of my life and didn't know at first how to find it, or even if I ever would. Yet I have remained committed to discovering it, and now I can honestly say that I'm getting more comfortable being naked on that glacier!

How can one be free and yet able to live with discomfort? I have learned that standing naked is staying in your own truth without insisting that others conform to your values. In fact, it matters very little if others laugh at you, turn away, or misunderstand you as long as you're standing in your "naked" truth. What is true for me may be different from what it is for you.

Finding out what truth means for each of us is the real journey. As the poet T. S. Eliot so beautifully articulated:

> We shall not cease from exploration
> And the end of all our exploring
> Will be to arrive where we started
> And know the place for the first time.
> (Eliot, "Little Gidding," Verse V)

I used to feel that I was very different from other people—I carried a lot of emotional pain and thought everyone must surely be aware of how much discomfort I felt! Everyone else was more beautiful, luckier, and happier than me. On top of that, I felt ashamed of my pain, which added even more discomfort.

Now I see that standing naked on the glacier is being on top of the pain and realising that it gives us a grand view. Climbing up the glacier is overcoming the blame-game programming that limits our living truly authentic lives. Finally, we realise that the glacier is the pain that has brought us to this point of awareness, and we are grateful.

I'm aware that everyone carries some degree of unresolved pain from the blame-game programming, and I'm now able to take this knowledge back into the world and help others to overcome the suffering created by these stories. I know that I'm not alone in carrying pain, and I now feel an immense commonality with everyone I meet.

However, being naked isn't easy at first. Expressing what's really happening in us when emotional pain is present can be quite challenging. Communicating our feelings while remaining non-blaming is truly being authentic. We learn to own up to our responsibility for the pain—not that we alone did it, but we can take responsibility for our healing. No one else is going to do it for us—this is the reality and the opportunity of life!

Remember earlier in the book we discussed a complaining culture—that is, how can we improve life if we don't complain about what's wrong? I promised to answer that question, and maybe you've already figured out the answer. But in case you haven't, here's my suggestion.

If we believe that someone or something about the world is not meeting our expectations, then what do we actually believe? Is it that we have the right view of the world? Are we not using should-or-should-k(not) programming? What if we saw it differently? What if we simply saw that the people or circumstances we were criticising had values and thought programs that were different from ours? Could we perhaps be more responsible in declaring what our values are and then asking if others might like to meet them as long as they don't compromise their own?

Being naked is being willing to accept that others may not share our values while remaining willing to state ours openly and respectfully, without expectations that other people's values *must* conform to ours. In fact, we might just like to know what theirs are—to see them intellectually and emotionally naked also and to appreciate the differences and similarities between their views and ours.

As we become at ease with being emotionally naked, then we don't really need the world to conform to our values, as we feel okay just as we are! Of course, sharing what's important to us is a natural act, and we do it with dignity and full awareness that other people may disagree. This is one of the miracles of becoming naked—we see fewer problems and more naked and authentic people underlying what we would normally have labeled as problems. All of the events and people that we generally label as problems are simply expressions of what doesn't meet our values, and if we saw the problems in that way, it would cause us so much less pain.

Modern society discourages us from being naked, being vulnerable, showing emotions, and sharing our real thoughts. Now I'm not encouraging anyone to be disrespectful of others, as part of being naked is our awareness and respect for other people, just as we are aware of our own needs and feelings. Naked is being respectful both of ourselves and of others at the same time! Whew, that sounds like a big ask, doesn't it?

It takes practice, practice, and more practice, but hey, isn't that what life's for? Why not try something new and see how it goes?

While you're practicing at revealing who you are with great dignity, keep this in mind. You will feel vulnerable and want to blame someone when you don't feel accepted. This is again normal, and if you are feeling this way, then the recommended medication is to forgive yourself and the other person.

Forgiveness is one of the most fundamentally important teachings, especially when we're releasing blame-game programming. We carry enormous amounts of guilt and blame around like they are family jewels, when, in fact, they are like sacks of stinking crap that really need to be ploughed into the garden. Whatever stories are haunting our minds, hanging around like ghosts that won't leave, please pay attention to them in a kind and direct way and then seek to feel underneath for the judgements and feelings that lie buried.

Let's assume that your partner has just told you that he was having an affair with a younger, richer, and better looking woman. You then became so angry that you took all his belongings and burned them in a big heap, because that felt right at the time. Did the anger really go away? Probably not, because there is now a new layer of judgement that has been added to the story: "You should k(not) have burned the stuff."

If you stay on that pathway, you'll end up very bitter, and yet it doesn't feel authentic to just forgive your partner. The first stage of becoming authentic is to look deeply into the initial rage and feel what is behind the sense of anger. Maybe you're actually angry at yourself because of the extra time spent at work during the past year. Maybe you had just assumed that your partner was okay about your absences from home. So, you begin to feel a deeper sadness in knowing that you wished you'd been more connected with your relationship.

Taking time to go under the initial feelings is good practice at being vulnerable. Emotional relief comes as you start to unravel the story: he should not have done that, and I should not have done this—meaning you would have liked it if things had happened another way, because you value (fill in blank). You might even attempt to talk to the other person about what happened and seek a mutual understanding of one another's reasons while remaining empathetic to the emerging feelings in yourself and also in your former partner.

Please remember that forgiveness doesn't mean we approve of the behaviour. It simply says we understand the behaviour was based on a mental model that couldn't reconcile dueling needs. In doing so, we're recognising the fallibility of our beliefs and cultural programming and realising that we try our best to do what seems right at the time. Over time, we may even be able to comprehend that most people's mental programming is in the driver's seat; therefore, their actions don't require forgiveness but simply an understanding that they "know not what they do."

Becoming comfortable in our vulnerabilities is a major shift in how we normally operate, which is to protect ourselves from what we fear. Judgement has become the shield that our egos use to create a sense of power. Yet, the stories we so often tell ourselves are simply barriers to our authentic power, which exists when we live as completely undefended and open human beings.

Be naked, be forgiving is allowing yourself to be vulnerable. As you understand how your stories create pain for yourself, you can easily forgive (and even move beyond forgiveness) and into inner peace.

Life Is a Flow, Let It All Go

If our authentic lives exist as a flow that allows thought and emotion to arise naturally and without judgement, then letting go of moralising judgement is the key to maintaining a feeling of love, joy, and acceptance. My experience tells me that releasing judgements and expectations is the final and necessary step in moving towards an authentic life.

Blame-game thinking limits our access to this natural flow. By learning to loosen up our habitual stories, we can begin to live freer and more unlimited lives. What if life were unfolding perfectly? If so, then the more we felt free to accept the experiences that arise over time, the greater the sense of contentment we'd feel. If we could feel that way regardless of the circumstances, I'd say that we would have reached the peak of human experience.

To allow something new to enter our lives, we must first learn to let go. The Chinese character for letting go is the same as the character for letting in. Until we release our limited sense of ourselves, we cannot welcome in a more expansive way of seeing who we really are.

A first step in releasing our limitations is to start with the thought that we are already enough just as we are right now. Our sense of deficiency is in itself a limitation. Why not try seeing ourselves as wonderful, amazing, already just perfect—without becoming obsessed about it? Let us imagine what it is like just to know that we have nothing to prove or anyone to impress. In fact, everything we do we could do just for the pure enjoyment of it.

Instead of wanting more, let what there is be enough. Instead of seeing a lack, let's see ourselves as full. Instead of feeling that our lives are impoverished, let's see them as incredibly abundant.

So, our sense of abundance must start in our hearts and minds; we must embrace the understanding that we are naturally abundant and whatever we're seeking is already present in us. This is beautifully illustrated by *The Wizard of Oz*, which is my favourite movie and was originally a well-loved children's book. The three companions of Dorothy, besides her dog, Toto, are the Scarecrow, the Lion, and the Tin Man. All of them believe, including Dorothy, that they are lacking an essential characteristic that, if they had it, would make them feel complete.

At the end of the story, the Wizard gives each of them a medal indicating that they possess this trait in great abundance. For the Tin Man, it's feelings; for the Lion, courage; and for the Scarecrow, intellectual reasoning. Of course, they had these traits all along, and the Wizard simply presented them with their own capacity to see it for themselves.

So when we release our feelings of inadequacy, shame, guilt, and impoverishment, we are allowing a space for touching the abundant and already good part of ourselves. Maybe we could do a spring cleaning of our minds and hearts on an annual basis.

Why are we afraid to let go of old beliefs about our lives and the world? Because they give us the comfort of knowing what to expect: the same old struggles and dramas that we seem to invite regularly into our days and nights. Eventually, though, we may become tired of the soap opera script that we've co-written and choose one that is in accordance with our authentic nature.

Letting go is not about giving up or choosing to be neutral about life. It is a conscious choice to begin releasing our egos' grip on our view of life and begin sensing options through our whole being. Maybe we could stop thinking that we're right all the time and yet still remain true to our sense of what is important to us.

Can we imagine what that might look like if everyone started practicing "maybe I'm not right" in their thoughts and words? Wouldn't it be refreshing to hear a politician say that an opponent was right, and he might be wrong!

I think we'd all start trusting that person if we felt he was genuine.

Also, we can create a lot more harmony in our daily interactions if we drop our sense of rightness. It's not about letting people bully us but rather about choosing not to engage in arguments from a sense of proving or defending ourselves. The same approach can apply to our own self-reflections. Why torture ourselves over insignificant decisions and actions? If we do our best, well, then that is enough. We can learn, move on, and be gentle in our thoughts. We can keep good intentions in everything we do, and even if things don't turn out exactly as we desired, we can remember that we are practicing the art of self-empathy and love.

Let go of expectations of yourselves and keep an open mind as to what is possible for you to think, be, and do. That means focusing on what you want, yet not becoming too worried about when or how it arrives. Remember to trust!

Let go of expectations about others, as they have their own journeys, and you are not here to be their guidance counselor. If they want advice, then let them ask. Otherwise, let them make the choices they need to make. Of course, remember that you can probably find a strategy that meets everyone's needs if you are open to hearing the desires of others.

Let go of fear. I know that this is not exactly straightforward, as we're highly sensitized to protecting our bodies and our fragile egos. However, if someone says a nasty word to you, then perhaps you can see it as a badly worded cry for help. Generally, people simply want to get rid of their own pain, and in doing so, they often trigger pain in others. If you begin seeing the world this way, you might let go of your habitual complaining about other people and see them as the wounded and deeply good beings that they are (and that you are too).

Life is a flow, let it all go is about releasing your limited sense of yourself, in order to allow space for the expansive and authentic being that you truly are.

Practices for Chapter 4

Release: Let Go to Let Your Authentic Life Flow

Practice 1

1. Place a few big signs in several places in your home and in your office that simply say "TRUST."

2. Then, each day write down in your journal any feelings, thoughts, and insights that emerge in regard to what trust means to you.

Practice 2

1. When you feel hurt by the actions or words of another person, try talking to yourself first with the words, "I feel X, because I need/would like Y." For example, "I feel hurt, because I would like more consideration of my time."

2. Then speak those words to someone, even if it isn't the person who was involved in the initial episode. Notice how the different choice of words gives you a new experience and then attempt to choose those words that feel most open, flowing, and life giving.

Practice 3

Sit quietly for several minutes while your mind relaxes and then ask yourself these questions:

1. Is there anyone in your life who you feel you cannot forgive? Why not? If you did forgive, what would that mean for you? Perhaps you have an unfulfilled need that is important for you to know and have that need met before it is easy to forgive. What can you do right now that would let you fulfill that need?

2. Have you forgiven yourself for behaviours that you may have regretted? Why not? If you did, what would that mean for you?

CHAPTER 5

Living an Authentic Life

I recently watched the *The Power of Myth*, a wonderful 1980s American television series in which Bill Moyers interviews Joseph Campbell, the articulate and inspiring scholar of religion and mythology. When I was in my mid-twenties, this series was shown on the Public Broadcasting Station in the United States, and I remember being completely enthralled when listening to Campbell. In viewing him today, I am equally impressed with Campbell's insightful ability to illustrate how the divergent cultural myths and religions of the world all indicate a similar meaning.

At one point in the episode I watched, Moyers asks Campbell, "Are we looking for meaning in life?"

Campbell, in his inimitable style, smiles and says, "I think people are not looking for meaning but rather for the experience of being fully human."

I was immediately in agreement with him, as I've often wondered about meaning and felt it didn't quite capture what I was looking for in my life.

What is the experience of being fully human? Perhaps living an authentic life is similar to what Campbell called "following our bliss." We are each endowed with a particular and unique set of mental, physical and emotional characteristics that create our personalities. Yet, in discovering our own sense of what it means to be fully human, we find that our personalities are lenses through which the source of our authentic natures can flow. We no longer see ourselves as autonomous individuals acting solely from our mental thought processes, which are primarily not of our own making.

How do we live more fully in the flow of our authentic nature? There are, I believe, natural laws that govern how we can receive this flow more fully, as described by sages, mystics, and enlightened beings throughout history. These individuals came to know their authentic selves through their own efforts at releasing societal conditioning and allowing the natural unfolding of their feelings and thoughts—without judgement.

I am a novice at learning these principles that govern an authentic life, and I am continually finding resources and people who assist me in deepening my understanding and putting them into practice. Throughout these pages, I have provided an overview of what I understand thus far about these natural principles and how cultural blame-game programming can block access to the ease of living authentically. This book is intended as guidance for using these key insights in practical ways that may be useful for you. Please explore and expand what I have provided here, rather than assuming that I can provide you with a comprehensive approach to living an authentic life.

Just before I found myself unknowingly slipping into the black hole of depression, I felt this powerful and raw desire to be authentic. At that critical moment, I established a strong intention to find out what it meant to live a fully authentic life. Until then, I felt that I'd lived without being fully whom I wanted to be. The depression was like a collapsing of my faulty world view, and although it created a great deal of pain for me during that period, it was simply a consequence of my programming reaching its futile endpoint. I could not be authentic and continue living and thinking from the blame-game programming I had learned.

I know that in reading this book, you have also chosen to release this cultural programming and open yourself to rediscovering your true nature.

So, remember to be brave. Try new things. Meet new and inspiring people. Allow feelings. Listen to yourself. Speak from your heart. Set clear intentions. Visit a forest and ask a tree a question. Listen for answers in the words of the next song. Let go of expectations. And most of all, be kind to yourself.

I believe that once we set clear intentions to live fully authentic lives, nothing will (or can) prevent us from obtaining what is naturally ours. At the end of this book are suggested resources that may be of further help to you. (See Bibliography.)

Enjoy the journey returning to your true home.

About the Author

Elaine K. Harding, PhD., is a born-again entrepreneur whose Authentic Leadership and Authentic Career programs reveal and develop the unique purpose that exists within every individual so that everyone can realise his or her highest potential. Her greatest achievement to date has been to discover that the great American dream is in need of a serious makeover.

You can contact Elaine through her website at www.thrivabilityconsulting.com.au.

Bibliography

Barks, Coleman, trans. *The Essential Rumi*. New York: HarperCollins Publishers, 2004.

Brach, Tara. *Radical Acceptance: Embracing Your Life with the Heart of a Buddha*. New York: Bantam Dell, 2003.

Brennan, Barbara Ann. *Hands of Light: A Guide to Healing Through the Human Energy Field*. New York: Bantam Dell, 1987.

Brennan, Barbara Ann. *Light Emerging: The Journey of Personal Healing*. Pp. 22-23. New York: Bantam Dell, 1993.

Brooks, Michael. 2012. Does Consciousness Create Reality? *New Scientist*: 215 (2884): 42-44.

Damasio, Antonio R. *Descartes' Error: Emotion, Reason, and the Human Brain*. New York: HarperCollins Publishers, 1994.

D'Ansembourg, Thomas. *Being Genuine: Stop Being Nice, Start Being Real*. California: PuddleDancer Press, 2007.

Eliot, T. S. "Little Gidding—Verse V." Accessed on July 2, 2013 at: http://www.columbia.edu/itc/history/winter/w3206/edit/tseliotlittlegidding.html.

Rosenberg, Marshall B. *Nonviolent Communication: A Language of Life, Second Edition.* California: Puddle Dancer Press, 2003.

Tolle, Eckhart. *The Power of Now: A Guide to Spiritual Enlightenment.* Hachette Australia, 2004.